To Betty

When I Was a Kid

When I Was a Kid

Growing Up in Nashville
From the '40s to the '70s

TOM HENDERSON III

To our Almighty for placing me in a time period that was,
and will be, like no other we will ever witness again.

*

To my wonderful sisters, parents and grandparents,
who brought me up in a loving home environment
where I was instilled with exceptional moral and character
values—values which I, unfortunately, did not always practice
but ones that I always remembered.

*

To all of the neighbors, friends, dogs, places, things and people I
came in contact with during the 1940s, '50s, '60s and '70s.

*

To my girlfriend, who, back in "The Summer of Love" in 1967,
saved me from a directionless future by selecting me
to be her husband.

*

To my children, grand children and all of those who will follow.

CONTENTS

FOREWORD

Back when Allen Forkum was trying to decide whether to launch a monthly newspaper that would focus on Nashville nostalgia and history, he said his main concern was whether there would be a steady source of material to publish. When he asked me to suggest a few people who might be regular contributors to the paper, the first person I mentioned was Tom Henderson. I told Allen that although Tom wasn't exactly a writer or a historian, he had a profound love, almost a passion, for a time that had nearly disappeared in Nashville—a time in which most Nashvillians who were at least 50 years old had grown up. When the initial issue of The Nashville Retrospect appeared in July 2009, it contained Tom's first article, and his articles have enriched each subsequent issue.

Month after month Tom has chronicled Nashville as it was from the late 1940s, when he was a toddler, until the early 1970s, when he was a young man. He has described, with a precision that future historians will likely cherish, what it was to grow up in a middle-class home in the Upper South during the years that followed World War II. Memories from those years move outward from his home on Cantrell Avenue and expand across the surrounding neighborhood like concentric ripples moving across the surface of a pond, and those ripples ultimately encompass the entire city and the experiences of many of its older native residents.

There is, beneath the surface of the author's memory, a sense of how much has been lost from the neighborhoods of Nashville, and from the neighborhoods of America, since the mid-1900s. We are constantly told that, thanks to its rapidly rising population and its booming economic growth, Nashville has become one of the nation's "it" cities. This book would contend that Nashville was a different example of an "it" city back when so much of its open land was not yet covered with housing developments, back when its quiet streets were not yet too congested for children to safely ride their bicycles, and back when its children could roam its neighborhoods without their parents being concerned for their well-being. "When I Was a Kid" is more than a look back at our collective past; in many respects it is a look back at a time that no longer exists.

But there is so much to celebrate—from the remembered rhythms of childhood when we spent days at home with our mothers and did yard work with our fathers, to the intricate fabric of how it was to go on family vacations and celebrate Christmas, to the intimate flavor of going to the neighborhood drugstore or barbershop or movie theatre, and to what it was like to have been a teenager in the early 1960s when rock 'n' roll, and high school combos, reigned supreme. "When I Was a Kid" takes us back to a time that was not only different, but that was, in many ways, superior to what kids experience today. When Mark Twain wrote "My Boyhood Dreams," he included a sentence that brings Tom Henderson's book to mind: "Ah the dreams of our youth, how beautiful they are, and how perishable."

Paul Clements

PREFACE

What you are about to read in this book is my first collection of personal stories, intertwined with history, that initially appeared in the wonderful historical newspaper The Nashville Retrospect. I wrote from what I remembered as a young child growing up in the south, beginning in the 1940s, all the way through the 1950s, 1960s and into my late 20s and 30s of the 1970s. I recently realized that specific events and recollections of those times were usually written about in generalities or on Internet "Do you remember when?" postings, without much regard for detail or personal input. Those stories resided in the minds of ordinary citizens like you and me. One of my goals in writing this book was to include the memories of people (including me) who were living during those times, memories that, years from now, if not put on paper, would have otherwise been lost forever.

"When I Was a Kid" will convey to you the feeling of what life was like during those years. I intentionally tried to relate each episode in the most favorable way, avoiding, for the most part, the more depressing events of that era. It is meant to be an uplifting read. Even though it is set in the suburbs of what is now called Woodmont Hills, in the southwestern part of Davidson County in Nashville, Tenn., the scene could have been anywhere in a small- to medium-sized town in America, particularly if you were a white, middle-class child labeled a "Baby Boomer."

"When I Was a Kid" is illustrated with personal and vintage photos, along with first-hand accounts from many folks who lived through those years. As you navigate each chapter, you will learn things about me and my upbringing in what I refer to as "the best of times." There are anecdotes, adventures and life lessons that will make you laugh, blush and maybe even shed a tear. Although "When I Was a Kid" did not start out as an autobiography, it seems to fit into that category. As a result, some names have gone unmentioned, to protect the guilty.

The chapters are laid out in no particular order, and it is designed that way. By doing this, the memory will be constantly jogged and not allowed to "hang out" in a certain time period. One chapter will be about teenage boys in the early 1960s driving around in a massive snow storm with too much time on their hands, and the next one might flash back to the days when children walked or rode their bikes to their neighborhood grade school in the 1950s. You will understand what kids went through attending "mandatory" dance lessons and then be thrust back to family vacations in automobiles with no air conditioning. You will read about 1969 from my perspective in one chapter and in another recall the Christmas of 1956. Remember the feel of walking to the local drugstore on a summer Saturday afternoon and what fun it was to go to the drive-in movies on a Friday night? What about those Doo Wop and make-out songs? They are in here as well.

I have had friends say, "I don't care about the past; I am just looking to the future." That is all well and good, but it has been found that nostalgia can soothe the soul. It helps older folks with no real future ahead realize that their life has been well spent, and it can challenge their mind to remember the times, especially the good ones, they had back in their youth. For those of us on the backside of things, we can still get together and reminisce about the good old days and think that maybe there is hope for the future—just maybe.

Whether you were a kid or a parent back in the mid-20th century, or if you are just a young person trying to get a fix on how your folks and grandparents grew up, or even someone wanting to learn about a time period long gone, then "When I was a Kid" is for you. Hearing about those days is one thing, but reading about it from someone who went through it is quite another.

For me, "When I Was A Kid" relates some of the best of times. I hope for you it will, too.

When I Was a Kid

CHAPTER 1

Going to the Drive-ins

IT ALL started in a New Jersey driveway at the home of Richard Hollingshead Jr. In the early 1930s, he mounted a 1928 projector atop the hood of his car. He nailed a screen between trees in his backyard and placed a radio behind it for sound.

In 1933 Hollingshead and three others opened the first drive-in movie theater on Crescent Boulevard in Camden, N.J. He named the theater, oddly enough, Drive-In Theatre and showed the comedy film "Wives Beware," starring Adolphe Menjou, charging 25 cents per person, one dollar maximum per car.

By 1948 drive-in theaters had increased in popularity so much that Edward Brown opened up the first "fly-in" in Asbury Park, N.J. It held 500 cars with the last row reserved for 25 aircraft. In the 1950s, Mobile, Ala., also had a fly-in called the Air-Sho Fly-In.

Drive-ins hit their peak in the 1950s and early 1960s. Post-war suburbia and the economy flourished, patriotism abounded, and the family was the centerpiece of the times. The Baby Boom era took off, and citizens vacationed with road trips in their American-made automobiles. People loved their cars and enjoyed showing them off.

But just like today, going out in the evening with several kids was a problem. And who likes the extra cost of a babysitter? The drive-in provided a perfect solution. Parents loaded up children, some in their pajamas, stocked their station wagon with blankets and food, and headed off to the nearest drive-in for an evening of family fun without having to pay a babysitter. Drive-ins were so popular that playgrounds, some accompanied by pony rides and carnival-like atmospheres, became part of the scene. Opening of the

*The Crescent Drive-In, located at Murfressboro Road and Thompson Lane, is pictured here in a
1957 Nashville Banner photo. "The Girl Can't Help It" starred Jayne Mansfield.* (Nashville Public
Library, Nashville Room)

gates prior to darkness enabled youngsters to frolic about the grounds before
the feature began. At their pinnacle over 5,000 drive-ins existed in America,
some with auto capacity of 2,000 or more.

Nashville was blessed with several drive-in theaters, all opening from
1948 to the mid-1950s.

The Crescent Drive-In at the corner of Murfreesboro Road and
Thompson Lane was the first in 1948 and billed itself as the "County's first
outdoor picture playhouse." Its 30-foot-by-40-foot screen lit up the sky at the
premier with "Thunderhead, Son of Flicka." The cost was 40 cents for adults.
Ages 6 to 12 were only 12 cents, and under 6 got in free. The newspaper pro-
mo released this statement from the management: "We will constantly study
the family likes and dislikes in screen entertainment in an effort to present
programs with maximum appeal." Its marquee was a huge tower displaying a
neon crescent moon with stars all around. It was quite a site.

In the early days, Walt Disney movies such as "Lady and the Tramp" and
"Snow White" were featured, and adventures and westerns were also shown
with regularity, to entice families with small children.

Drive-in shows usually opened with a greeting followed by a newsreel, a "short" and a cartoon before the main attraction began, usually in glorious Technicolor.

The Colonial on Old Hickory Boulevard opened April 1, 1950, and boasted a 70-foot screen. The Skyway on Dickerson Road also opened April 1 with Zane Grey's "Red Canyon," and advertised that baby bottles would be warmed for free. These were followed by the Lebanon Road Drive-In, the Warner Park Drive-In (at Vaughn's Gap Road and Highway 100) and the Bel-Air Drive-In (at 5900 Charlotte Ave. across from Richland School). The Montague on Gallatin Road and the Bordeaux on Highway 41 (Clarksville Highway) were popular, each having an auto capacity from 500 to 750.

These outdoor venues were designed so that everyone had a clear view of the screen. Some were elevated from front to rear, like Warner Park, and usually had a concession stand centrally located for convenience. Eventually intermission trailers, featuring dancing hot dogs and popcorn boxes, were shown between movies. Goodies ranged from pizza to ice cream, with the pizza slices tasting much like the box they came in. This was not gourmet dining.

Finding the way back to your car with snacks on a crowded Saturday night was often a challenge. Did you park in the third row or fourth? Was it the eighth or the seventh car from the end? Eventually you made it back, balancing all of the tasty treats in those sturdy containers.

The No. 1 song in 1950 was the Platters' "Twilight Time," and it would have been a fitting song to play at drive-ins just as dusk was closing in. The Platters also appeared in "The Girl Can't Help It" starring the vivacious Jayne Mansfield, which played at the Crescent Drive-In in 1957. Little Richard performed the title song. Drive-ins were so popular that 12-year-old Dodie Stevens sang about going to a drive-in in her 1959 hit "Pink Shoe Laces," and so did Nat King Cole in his 1963 hit "Those Lazy Hazy Crazy Days of Summer."

Most theaters came with in-car heaters and utilized a rectangular speaker box that you pulled inside, providing not only pre-movie tunes but also announcements from management. Often these devices were defective, causing disgruntled moviegoers to relocate to another site. It was not uncommon to drive away forgetting to remove the speaker.

Late arrivers often forgot to turn off their headlights, causing a barrage of horn honks and obscenities. This was especially annoying if that auto parked directly behind your vehicle, silhouetting you and your sweetie in a compromising pose. These "submarine races" (an endearing term for those parked cars with amorous shenanigans taking place on the inside) were often disrupted by a flashlight-wielding, pimply-faced usher who would tap on the window to make sure all heads were above seat level. (It should be noted that all ushers were not pimply-faced.)

Horns blared and lights really let loose when the film would break or the feature started late.

Teens and young adults drove with their dates and friends, showing off their own cars (or those given to them by their parents). Gates opening early allowed proud drivers to cruise down each row slowly, showcasing their rides. Those already in their viewing spots often watched as the cars motored by. Kids fortunate enough to have a convertible were able to sit on the top of the trunk with feet hanging down on the back seat, allowing for a prime view. Others either remained inside the car or sat on their hoods. Of course, if you had a date, the back row was preferred as it offered a more secluded observation post.

Underage drinking was also highly suspected. Fortunately, I was never called to testify.

The 1960s brought with it the age of television and information just as the Baby Boomers began driving. These once pajama tikes, who fell asleep after a Walt Disney movie, now wanted more than what appeared on the surface, whether it was appropriate or not.

Theater owners, adjusting to the culture and demographic change, shifted their programming to campier, more revealing themes. Classic horrors such as "Attack of the Giant Leeches" and "I Was a Teenage Werewolf," released in 1956, were replaced by B-movies such as "Drag Strip Girl," "Dementia 13," "Blood Feast" and a tidal wave of beach movies, such as "Muscle Beach Party," "The Horror of Party Beach" and "Girls on the Beach."

Drive-ins also began showcasing triple features of vampire, occult and risqué themes to entice their rapidly changing market. On April 2, 1964, the Skyway lured young adults with the highly-acclaimed films "Kiss of the

The Bel-Air Drive-In on Charlotte Avenue advertises adult entrainment, in particular the 1964 Italian "shockumentary" "Weird, Wicked World." (Nashville Metro Archives)

Vampire," "Fiend Without a Face" and "The Haunted Strangler." Later that month the management followed those stellar flicks with the hormonal "White Slave Ship" and "Female Jungle," in Colorscope no less.

Not to be outdone, the Lebanon Road Drive-in countered with the well-endowed June "Boom Boom" Wilkerson starring in "The Bell Boy and the Playgirls." Then Warner Park jumped into the fray, strutting out famous foreign nudie sensation Bridget Bardot in some of her much ballyhooed performances.

Cruising around one spring night in 1964—with the AM radio playing everything from Major Lance to "Warm California Sun," the instrumental "Wild Weekend," "Surfing Bird" and songs by the new English groups Dave Clark Five, Herman's Hermits and The Beatles—several of us high-schoolers decided to go see the stomach-turning flick "2,000 Maniacs" playing at the Crescent Drive-In. It featured June 1963 Playboy's Playmate-of-the-Month Connie Mason and centered around a southern town enacting gruesome revenge on northern tourists for Civil War transgressions. The classic line in that hack fest was "I reckon we got ourselves the makin's for a barbeque!"

Our first mistake was to attempt to sneak in a classmate George Leonard without paying. The second was to have him lie down on the back floorboard

The Skyway Drive-In on Dickerson Road advertises the 1952 adventure film "The Wild North" on its marquee. (Nashville Metro Archives)

covered up by a few letter jackets and several D-minus theme papers. George was 6 foot 3 inches. Great minds we were. The usual way was to hide in the trunk, but theater management had caught on to this caper. Approaching the entrance I collected enough money for three of us and slowed as the usher peered out of the ticket booth. Using his flashlight to pan the back seat, he noticed the unusual pile of jackets and loose-leaf notebook paper, and George's protruding feet. A sense of humor allowed us to proceed, for the forgiving young usher asked if I wanted to pay for the pair of shoes sticking out. I replied that I preferred not, but that if it meant no admission or the movie police would come to investigate, then there would be no problem accounting for the shoes. We were waved in and witnessed a classic presentation of a gory B-movie.

By the end of the 1960s and into the 1970s, the post-WWII euphoria and overwhelming fascination of doing everything in a car began to wane. Baby Boomers, aging into their 20s and beyond, fueled a pronounced cultural and moral shift that cut into drive-in attendance. Families quit attending, so theater playgrounds were disassembled. The increasing popularity of television and rock 'n' roll, the construction of multiplex cinemas, and the realization by theater owners that their huge open areas could be sold for large profits didn't help either.

Outdoor theater managers, unable to acquire first-run movies that were going to the large indoor chains, were relegated to showing triple features of those B-grade films and worse that began surfacing in the 1960s. Then came bucket car seats, cable TV and VCRs in the late 1970s and '80s, further diminishing the drive-in popularity. The 5,000 or so dwindled to less than 400 by the 1980s. The heyday was over.

The Nashville run of some 36 years was a good one. The last to succumb was the Skyway. It managed to hang on until 1984, when the lights went out for good, and the drive-in theater era in our city came to a close.

Those star-filled nights of the 1950s— in pajamas watching a family film and then falling asleep in the back seat as a little kid—are now a distant memory. The anticipation of slowly reaching your arm around Peggy Sue and hoping to have her slide across the long front seat while watching a classic on the outdoor screen is something not easily forgotten.

It was a simpler, bygone era of my often misspent youth. I can still hear the Platter's singing "for now it's Twilight Time" as the projector illuminates the massive outdoor screen with the final words: "The Management Thanks You For Your Patronage...THE END."

Chapter 2

The Home Coal Furnace

MANY HOMES in Nashville built prior to the end of WWII were constructed with basements. More often than not those basements came with a built-in coal furnace complete with an accompanying bin to house the black, walnut-sized chunks. Other homes used either gas or oil furnaces as their main source of heat. However, the most prevalent heating source from the 1930s to the mid-1960s was coal. It was cheap, put out lots of heat and was readily available.

The coal bin in our basement was directly under my bedroom. We had a full basement accessible from the inside through the breakfast room and from the outside by several steep, twisting concrete steps that were almost hidden by the back porch and various shrubberies.

Entering from the breakfast room, a wooden flight of stairs with a hand-rail led one to the underside of our house. After the first few steps I could usually tell if my mom was washing clothes, for there would be a pleasing smell of fresh laundry detergent. But most of the time a dusty, somewhat damp odor could be detected.

In the basement was a narrow corridor bordered on either side by a rock foundation. A single naked light bulb hung from the ceiling with a string for activation. Past that light a few feet was another naked light bulb between a huge box-looking structure that was our coal furnace and the bin where the coal was stored. The bin was some eight feet high at the entrance with an additional two to three feet in height on the back shelf inside the bin. It was some 20 feet in length. During the day coal dust could be seen floating in a stream of light that originated from a rectangular window at the top of the bin. The window was just large enough for someone with lots of ambition to

The Kathy Hamilton coal barge was named after Cathy Hamilton, daughter of Fred Hamilton, who worked for the Nashville Coal Company (the spelling of "Kathy" was a mistake). Friends and family attended the 1953 launch at the Nashville Bridge Company on the river downtown. Front row (left to right): Buzzy Hamilton, Cathy Hamilton, Josh Ambrose, Rhea Sumpter, Billy Kuhn and Alex Slabosky. Back row: Billy Wilson, Diane Hall, David Sumpter, Tommy Henderson (the author), Patrick Wilson and Justin Wilson. Notice the low skyline compared to today; Nashville's first post-WWII skyscraper, the L&C Tower, would not be built until 1956. (Cathy Hamilton)

crawl through. My grade-school friends and I had quite a bit of ambition on numerous occasions. Clothes and faces would be covered in black when we emerged in our front yard. As a result of violating strict orders not to play in the coal bin, I became the unwilling recipient of several maternal switchings, none of which was pleasant or forgotten.

This window was the delivery portal for coal. Deliveries usually occurred in the warmer months (it was cheaper to buy in the summer) and attracted a host of neighbors who watched the coal truck back into our front yard and unload. Workers would assemble a long conveyor belt, insert it through the narrow window below my bedroom, then elevate the contraption. The coal was then shoveled from the truck onto the continuously moving belt. It was a noisy and lively operation that created quite a stir. The black pieces were deposited into our basement until the bed of the truck was empty. It was a big annual event and, as Nat King Cole's hit stated in 1952, "Unforgettable."

Cassetty Coal Company was our home coal deliverer. They were one of over 100 coal companies doing business in Nashville during the heyday of the coal furnace from the 1930s to the mid-1960s.

Saint Bernard Coal Company was another one that is remembered by young and old for its famous sign on Harding Road where today's entrance for Saint Thomas Hospital is located. The huge illuminated billboard featured a large St. Bernard dog in overalls with a top hat holding a piece of sudsy coal in one paw while the other paw moved back and forth over it, as if scrubbing. The caption said something to the effect, "We have the cleanest coal in town!" That large St. Bernard was prevalent in our minds in 1954, as it reminded us of the TV show "Topper." We were fascinated by the show mainly because of the plot line involving the invisibility of the supporting actors and their dog, a lovable St. Bernard named Neil.

My neighbors on Cantrell Avenue were the Hamiltons. Fred Hamilton worked for yet another coal enterprise, the Nashville Coal Company, and once named a coal-carrying barge after his daughter, Cathy, calling it the "Kathy Hamilton." To her chagrin, her first name was misspelled.

Our furnace required constant attention during cold months. This procedure in itself was labor-intensive. My father would descend the steps into the basement and grab a long-handled shovel sporting an exceptionally wide scoop with the sides turned up to prevent the coal from falling off. He would shovel the stoker rocks from the concrete floor of the coal bin and then empty them into a large steel bucket. He would then carry the fuel cells several steps to the stoker. The sound of the shoveling could be heard in every room of our house, thanks to our air duct system and wall vents. Once at the stoker box, he would hoist the bucket up and empty it. A large screw-like device would push the pellets into the furnace, where they were consumed by fire hot enough to melt stone, it seemed. Most of this procedure could have been avoided had we used lump coal. Lump coal could be dropped directly into the furnace—no shoveling or hoisting the bucket to the stoker. However, lump coal, often dumped in the homeowner's yard, was bulkier and had to be stacked. Therefore stoker coal became the preference of the majority of homeowners.

The coal burned according to what temperature was set on the thermostat. A built-in electric fan would circulate the hot air into the ducts and

Cassetty Coal Company executives in 1940 (left to right): Tilman Williams, Lewis Ervin, Fred J. Cassetty, Fred B. Cassetty and Hobson Byers. Cassetty Coal was located on 4th Avenue North across from Sulpher Dell. Behind the men are stacks of lump coal which, though heavy, could be put directly into a coal furnace, unlike the smaller coal used for stoking. (Fred Cassetty)

throughout the house. (My sisters said this fan was used to circulate air in summer to keep the house cool. There was no air conditioning in their early youth nor mine in the 1940s). Obviously the colder it was outside the faster the coal incinerated and the more often it needed "stoking."

Stoking the fire was just the initial step in maintaining the home coal furnace. Once the black coal was fully burned, large chunks of impurities were left over. These impurities manifested themselves in the form of irregular, grapefruit-sized "clinkers." Clinkers had to be removed on a regular basis or the furnace would not operate properly. Removing these white-hot objects was done with a long, thin, steel-handled contraption with a crab-like claw on one end and a lever that closed the claw on the other. After the furnace door was opened, the claw retriever was inserted into the flames, one hand twisting the lever while the other manipulated the pincher over a clinker. Once it was grabbed, you pulled the clinker out, placed it into a large steel bucket, and went after another one.

These clinkers piled up and were set outside for the garbage men. One would think that these residual rocks would be worthless. However, these pieces of melted ash were taken to various sites within the city, such as Vanderbilt and the V.A. Hospital. They were manually busted up and used for most of the school tracks during that era. Cinder tracks were quite prevalent, and if you ever fell on one you would never forget it. It took days to remove all those tiny cinders.

In 1960, as Fred Cassetty Jr. graduated from Vanderbilt, his father took him aside and told him that the coal business as he knew it, home delivery and all, was coming to an end. He advised young Fred to find another line of work. Tragically, his father died of a heart attack shortly after that talk. Fred Jr., at age 22, found himself in the coal business whether he liked it or not. He also never forgot his father's words, for his dad foresaw what the post-war housing boom in "suburbia" was doing and what was to follow. Homes started to be built without basements for the most part. The advent of cheap electric and gas heat operated by simply flipping a switch—instead of laboriously stoking fires and removing clinkers in a dingy basement—appealed to most homeowners. Pollution enforcement and strong-arm tactics by government officials with regard to fines and threats of closures forced many businesses to forgo the coal furnace route.

During cold months downtown Nashville was often barely visible due to all of the smoke generated by coal-burning businesses and homes alike. My sisters and I both remember flicking tiny black specs off of curtains, clothes and windowsills on a regular basis. Wearing white in the winter subjected one to the possibility of fashion malpractice.

Eventually, upgraded equipment became scarce, leaving many furnaces without adequate replacement parts or the personnel to service them. Nevertheless, our family maintained and utilized the old furnace into the early 1970s. Fred Cassetty continued to operate his at the family home until 1977—one of the last home coal furnaces to be used in our city.

Despite all the rigors and environmental concerns associated with our furnace, the positives far outweighed the negatives for a youngster like me in the early 1950s. Pollution and black specs did not bother me. To me it was an adventure to trek down the basement staircase with my dad, pull the strings to cut on the lights, and walk back to the coal bin where Dad would lift the iron handle and open the furnace door. Peering at the flames and watching him remove the white-hot clinkers while feeling the heat on my face was something special. Scaling the mountain of coal in the bin to get to the rectangular window was an experience in itself, especially with the risk of a tanned rear end looming. In particular, I will always remember going to bed in the dead of winter and hearing my father in the basement using the broad shovel to scoop coal from the concrete floor. The muffled sound of him depositing that coal into the steel bucket gave me a sense of security and well-being that would forever be imbedded in my mind. It was a wonderful, forever-gone childhood experience that is, for lack of a better word, unforgettable.

CHAPTER 3

Late December
Back in '63

THERE IS something about a snowfall that generates a feeling of excitement and goodwill that encompasses all ages, from the smallest children just becoming aware of their surroundings to the octogenarians in the waning years of life. During most of my life, prognostications of how much snowfall our city would have only added to the anticipation. There were even media contests based on guessing the date of the season's first significant snowfall. Old wives' tales, such as the number of fogs in August, the height or lack thereof of a hornet's nest and the width of a woolly worm's bands, have always played a large part in those meteorological predictions.

Just prior to Christmas in 1963, on Sunday, Dec. 22, Nashville recorded six inches of snow in six hours. As a teenager who never outgrew his childhood excitement over any mention of snow, I was ecstatic! My bedroom was on the second floor of our home on Cantrell Avenue, with windows facing both east and west. During snowfalls I would run to each end of my room to peer out and check on the mounting accumulation, especially on the east side, because my window air-conditioning unit served as a makeshift snow gauge. That vantage point also enabled me to observe the flakes reflecting down above our basketball court, thanks to two very tall light poles, which I always made sure were activated for any forecast of snow. When the wintry weather finally ended early on Monday the 23rd, Nashville had recorded over seven inches.

The only problem was that the temperature dropped to zero degrees, eliminating any extended outdoor fun. Oddly enough, the movie "Pyro" was playing at the downtown Paramount Theater. We could have used some of that heat.

Original caption from the Dec. 23, 1963, Nashville Banner: "A WHITE CHRISTMAS is the Nativity Scene in Centennial Park where camels and palm trees are snow-laden." (Nashville Public Library, Nashville Room, photo by Don Foster)

In 1963, WSM-TV moved into a new broadcast facility on Knob Hill. The weatherman on that station was Boyce Hawkins, who, along with side-kick Happy A. Clown, also doubled as Grandpa Moses on the afternoon kid-die show "Happy Town." I believe he stated that no more snow was expected for a while. No kid wanted to hear that. The old saying goes that if snow stays on the ground for more than three days you can expect another one. That crossed my mind as the white stuff lingered through Christmas thanks to the cold. It was not snowing on that day but it was still on the ground, making for a wonderful, festive holiday and nurturing hopes that another round was just around the corner.

The forecast for New Year's Eve, according to the Nashville Banner, was for four inches of snow in southern middle Tennessee, with lighter amounts expected in Nashville. Any mention of snow got the adrenalin moving. Late in the afternoon of Dec. 31, the sky had lowered considerably and the gray coldness that seemed to accompany frozen precipitation was prevalent throughout the area. By 7 p.m. the wet, heavy type began to come down and blanket everything.

The author's father, Tom Henderson, and the family pet, Kris Kringle, on Jan. 1, 1964.

I was planning to go out in my 1959 white Fiat 500, a tiny, lightweight, four-on-the-floor foreign vehicle that my parents told me I could use. No way I was to borrow their 1962 Chevy Impala, in light of my numerous speeding citations. It turned out to be a blessing in disguise, for the Fiat negotiated flawlessly during wintry conditions.

I left the house to the obligatory "be very careful driving and behave yourself" as my folks turned away from the "Jack Benny Show" just as Mr. Benny's house man, Rochester, spouted his weekly line, "Comin', Mister Benny!" I knew that my folks would ring in 1964 with Guy Lombardo and probably switch over at some point to laugh with my favorite funny man, Steve Allen, on "The Steve Allen Show."

I had no date for that New Year's Eve, through no one's fault but my own. So my next-door neighbor, friend and fellow celebrant for the evening became David Ligon, who had moved to Nashville from Ohio. He was hardly concerned about my lack of a girlfriend for the night as his courtship prowess also left him, shall we say, outside in the cold as well.

By 8 p.m. the roads were covered and visibility was reduced to a matter of yards. My Fiat, being so light, trekked across the varying terrain of Woodmont Hills in fine fashion.

Then came one of those once-in-a-lifetime moments. I was approaching the intersection of Lynnwood Boulevard and Hobbs Road, with snow coming straight down, when a bolt of lightning struck the telephone pole in a yard just across the street! An immediate clap of thunder further opened our eyes. I had never seen such an amazing phenomenon…lightning in a snowstorm!

Adding further excitement to the night, Fred Hart—a classmate and mutual friend of Dave and mine whom we had picked up earlier—reminded us that maybe we could spot the evasive Cat Burglar! This was an individual who had broken into 20 homes in the Green Hills and Woodmont areas within the past eight days. Local authorities penned the name because of his stealthiness; he left only footprints in the snow. They determined from the size of the imprints that he was a very large fellow, further adding to the mystique and intrigue. The criminal had recently forced his way into several houses on Valley Brook Road and one on Golf Club Lane. In one home lived two kids who attended the same school I did. This burglar took cash from their mother while she was still in the house!

Believing our detective skills were equivalent to Joe Friday of "Dragnet" and Kookie of "77 Sunset Strip," it was surmised we could possibly spot this guy and alert authorities. Now with a specific purpose for New Year's Eve, we drove through snow-covered main streets and negotiated back roads at breakneck speeds, sliding and spinning on our way to the crime areas while listening to music through the static of the Fiat's a.m. radio. We heard legendary disc jockey Noel Ball play "Popsicles And Icicles" by the Mermaids, "You Don't Have To Be A Baby To Cry" by the Caravells, "Walkin' The Dog" by Rufus Thomas, and the big make-out tune (for those who had a significant other) "Since I Fell For You" by Lenny Welch. "It's My Party" by Leslie Gore was also popular. Weeks earlier the play list also included "Santa Claus is Watchin' You" by Ray Stevens, who soon was to be Dave's new neighbor when he later moved to Lincoln Court.

We were reveling in the thrill of it all, listening to tunes and oblivious to the perils of motoring in such conditions (the consumption of several 12- and

16-ounce canned beverages may have also been a contributing factor).

The white flakes were so dense at this point that visibility was almost non-existent. My flimsy, single-bar wipers strained to move the piles of snow from one side of the windshield to the other. They were more or less useless, and unfortunately so was the detective work. The Cat Burglar eluded our grasp and remained on the loose. Good thing for him that things got worse for us.

I turned a corner and proceeded up Estes Road. Due to a less-than-adequate windshield defroster, I stuck my head out of the window to see the road, snowflakes sticking to my face and blowing hair. John R. (Richbourg) had just come on the air at WLAC 1510 for Ernie's Record Mart with his trademark line "Way Down South In Dixie." Dave was wiping off the passenger side window with the sleeve of his madras shirt. Fred was doing his best on the back window with one of my several failed Algebra tests, and I began using an old towel on the driver's side windshield.

All at once another vehicle came sliding down the hill toward us. There was a jarring crash as we were front-ended by the rear end of an out-of-control four-door sedan. The snowfall was so dense it was hard to tell the make or model. Soon a short, stocky, disheveled gentleman with a tan suit emerged into the wintry onslaught. His brown wing tips provided no traction in the powdery stuff; his feet slipped out from under him just as he managed to grasp the door handle. I exited from what I thought was a smashed-in Fiat 500. But we made a quick survey and concluded that neither vehicle was severely damaged. The man struggled back to his vehicle, re-started the engine and proceeded to spin his tires, going nowhere fast. Sensing that this kind soul could not negotiate the grade of Estes Road, we three good Samaritans braved the elements and physically pushed his car up the snow-covered street, making sure he could continue on his way. He thanked us profusely and gave me his business card. Other drivers were not as fortunate, for the ditches were strewn with abandoned autos. The snow depth was almost mid-tire level.

We continued our trek to nowhere, buffeted by the confetti-like downpour that was so bright headlights were not needed. People seemed to be out everywhere that night, just enjoying the huge snowstorm engulfing the city.

A collaborative decision was made to attempt a journey to the popular

The author (right) and his friend David Ligon are pictured on Jan. 2, 1964, one day after the big snow.

Warner Park Drive-In Theater on Highway 100, just to see what the storm was doing to the grassy areas and to observe the plight of the many moviegoers. We never made it, but I was sure autos were stranded as they tried to exit the hilly terrain of the outdoor venue. Being stuck would have been okay for some of those kids, as it was a noted spot to take your honey for some undisturbed "quality time." The movie being shown that night was "Splendor in the Grass" with Natalie Wood and Warren Beatty. Any splendor that night, I thought, would be done in snow, which more than likely played out at some point during the evening, either there or up on Nine Mile Hill less than a mile away. Incidentally, Warner Park Drive-In, having opened in 1956 with another outdoorsy title, "Picnic," advertised in the paper that in-car heaters were available. Not a bad device for such a wintry eve.

Later on, after meeting up with friends and throwing snowballs at various objects and other revelers, we eventually slipped and spun our way back home just in time to see Steve Allen usher in 1964. We opted out of Guy Lombardo's annual year-ending telecast.

On New Year's Day the snow diminished somewhat, leaving in its wake a record accumulation that remained on the ground for several more days, beautifying our neighborhoods and prolonging sledding for many young kids. My friends and I had just been an active part of the third biggest snowfall in Nashville history—10.2 inches! (Way back in 1892 we had 17 inches, and in 1929 a 15-inch beauty graced our community.)

Thinking back to the prior night, I remembered the business card given to me by the helpless motorist. I looked it over and realized that the name, Alex Schoenbaum, was synonymous with Shoney's Big Boy hamburger restaurants. Schoenbaum had begun by opening the Parkette drive-in restaurant in Charleston, W.V., in 1947, and in 1951 he changed the name to Shoney's, eventually teaming with Ray Danner of Nashville in 1971. The rest is history.

I remember him being a kind fellow and quite a solid-looking gent. Little did I know that he was a Grantland Rice All-American tackle at Ohio State from 1936 to 1938, just as my father was at Vanderbilt in 1931. (My friend Dave from Ohio would have asked for Schoenbaum's autograph had he known who he was.) Schoenbaum was a charitable person, donating millions to the Boy Scouts and The Salvation Army over his lifetime. Thirty-three years later, two days before Christmas, Mr. Schoenbaum passed away at age 81. I was glad we were on Estes Road that night to help him.

The Four Seasons' very last No. 1 hit said it all: "Oh What a Night, Late December back in '63." We rang in the New Year stalking the Cat Burglar, witnessed thunder and lightning during a record snowfall, and rescued the original Shoney's Big Boy from a slippery slope.

It was a night to remember but, as Dave later noted, "we didn't even get a free hamburger!"

CHAPTER 4

Riding Bikes

SOME SAY the origins of the bicycle date back to 1817. A German, Baron Karl Drais, invented an all-wooden "running machine" that could move more people at faster rates with less cost, upkeep and care than horse-drawn carriages and coaches. His "Hobby Horse" or "velocipede" (fast feet) was the first contraption with two wheels placed in a line. Riders sat on a leather seat and moved the piece of equipment forward with their feet. Roads were horrible, and collisions with unsuspecting pedestrians were frequent. In addition there were no brakes. It vanished quickly.

Through the late 1800s, "High Wheelers" and "Bone Shakers" became part of the scene. One can imagine how these rides felt. Tricycles and quadricycles were produced for women, eliminating the need to pull up skirts or expose underwear to take a ride. They came equipped with brakes and were much easier to operate.

In 1885 the Rover, the precursor to today's bikes, was introduced. Solid rubber tires were later replaced

The author on his Taylor Tot quadricycle in May 1948.

The store front of Bob's Bicycle Shop at 422 Broadway in the 1940s. Bike repairman Gordon Oldham prepares to make a delivery on a motorcycle with a sidecar converted to a hauling box. (Anne Husband)

with pneumatic ones by John Dunlop, making for a smoother ride. Ignatz Schwinn and Adolph Arnold began producing these "Safety Bikes" in 1894, contributing to the cycling mania of the "Gay '90s." At one point over 300 companies were making bicycles.

Unfortunately, the boom waned after 1898 as roads improved and the auto was introduced shortly thereafter. By the 1920s, bicycles were mainly seen as a kid's toy and took a back seat to the emerging auto industry.

In 1948 my folks purchased a rolling stroller for my leisure activity called a Taylor Tot. My model, according to collector Tom Murrah, was the Imperial. Movement was accomplished by leg action, similar to that used on the 1817 velocipede, thereby causing the mostly metal contraption to inch forward at mind-numbingly slow speeds. It was a safe way for toddlers to motor about.

A year or two later I found myself aboard a tricycle which had the same name as the "Gay Nineties" edition but was designed for both sexes. I pedaled around our home with sibling and parental supervision until the early 1950s. That is when the real fun began.

At age 6, I was ready to move to the next stage: a real bike. The first experiment was a hard-to-pedal model with two training wheels attached to the rear hub. Once I got the hang of it, the trainers came off. It took a while, but with plenty of Mercurochrome, gauze, and encouragement from the family, I was eventually able to stay upright. Around the age of 7 I became fairly accomplished and adult supervision slowly vanished. I was finally on my own.

Bikes could be bought at a number of locations in Nashville, but the store for bicycles, particularly Schwinns and motorbikes, was Bob's Bicycle Shop on Broadway. It was opened by Bob Couser in 1938, then sold to the Oberchain family. In 1941 Jack Tillman took over and, along with his daughter Anne and her spouse Charles Husband, ruled supreme in cycle sales and service until closing Christmas Eve 1976. It was originally located where Tootsie's Orchid Lounge is now and later moved across the street to 425 Broadway.

I remember traveling to Bob's in the 1950s and gazing up in wonderment at the many bikes hanging from the ceiling. They came with balloon tires, cantilever frames and all types of accessories. Each was marvelously painted to entice the young buyer.

The late 1950s to the early part of the 1960s was my bicycling heyday. Most everyone my age had a bike. The "Dog Days of Summer" were particularly bike worthy. Nothing much to do but jump on the freedom machine and take off. If I rode to my friend Andy's house and his mom said he had gone to Ed's, I would pedal down the street, cut through the Weavers' driveway, traverse several backyards, dodge the ever-present hedges and clotheslines, and look for several bikes lying next to the front door. We all knew what each other rode.

Sandlot baseball games in my neighborhood usually took place in Herbert's Field, at the Tompkins home, Woodmont School, or any large

The author at age 6 crashes in his back yard while learning to ride without training wheels.

Larry Herbert rides on the rear fender while Rob Skinner prepares to launch the bike at his home on Lynnbrook Road. Notice Skinner's rolled up right pant leg; that prevented it from getting caught in the chain. (Sam Herbert)

vacant lot. Riding the few blocks to get there to play ball while transporting equipment was often cumbersome, however, methods were developed to overcome it. First you would slide your Mickey Mantle glove (with the buttoned back strap) over the handlebar where it would hang freely. Next, your wooden Babe-Ruth-autographed bat would lie straight across those same bars with your fingers firmly gripping the bat ends while the thumbs grabbed the handlebars. An old baseball made new by white shoe polish in one pocket, bubble gum in the other, and ball cap on your head made steering a challenge but doable. Fortunately, most of us had coaster brakes without gears, so no other hand action was required. Negotiating steep hills with only one speed was a problem. We often had to stand up and pedal or just get off and walk. Riding your bike to football practice was another matter.

We all emulated older kids for their showmanship or what they did to their bikes. One of those kids was Sam Herbert, living only an open field away and just one year ahead of me, but close enough to be included in our group. He would ride to my house with reckless abandon, sliding sideways, slinging clusters of gravel and Indian money in our driveway, and usually yelling "Yipppp Piii!" His bikes were stripped to the bone and never new, mainly because they were handed down from older brother Charley. I used to get new bikes by default, as I had no older brother but two sisters. No girl bike for me. Sam's influence caused me to strip a new Schwinn down to the basics, resulting in severe buyer's remorse for my parents.

In order to mimic older kids who rode motorcycles, we regularly tied small semi-inflated balloons to our spokes. Only blowing them up halfway was essential to leave room to tie the ends. Baseball cards were also attached with wooden clothespins for added sound effects. Thousands of dollars worth of vintage collectibles were destroyed in this manner as were an inordinate number of cheap balloons.

Night cycling seemed to create an environment for us to push the limits. There was not much traffic in my area during this time and streets were generally quiet, as my neighborhood had yet to be annexed into the city. Regulations and overzealous developers had not yet made their mark on the neighborhood school or open lots. When suppertime ended, off we went. The breeze of the evening summer air in your face and hair (along with those pesky gnats), the sounds of katydids in the tall maples, coupled with a whip-poorwill or two on a telephone line gave us young lads a sense of freedom we had never before experienced. The distant echo of friends "playing out" resonated for blocks, so you could always tell if someone else was nearby. The aroma of cut grass and burning leaves was ever present. It seemed to be the norm back then and is a distant but pronounced memory of my youth and of those special times.

One of my more infamous nocturnal cycling maneuvers came unexpectedly one hot night in front of Paul Clements' home just four blocks away. Several of us would regularly ride the trails in a small thicket owned by the Barber family on Clearview Drive adjacent to Paul's. This was more like figure-eight racing without lights. It was fun, frightening and suspenseful. The lack of visibility and high probability of collisions with another bike, a friend's dog, or a young sapling, together with Sam's signature cries in the darkness, made the adventure more alluring. If you were fortunate enough to get through the trails unscathed, you would exit this small forest onto the narrow street and often blister it down a short hill to a ditch that, when

Kids' bikes are parked haphazardly on the curb of the Franklin Theatre in 1949. The scene was typical of neighborhood movie houses at the time. (Rick Warrick)

approached at a minimum speed, would propel you and your bike airborne before you landed safely in the yard.

This particular night I had negotiated the Barbers' thicket trail in fine fashion for the "umpteenth" time. I then wheeled at a breakneck clip (my unbuttoned shirt flapping against my back) down the street and headed directly for the trench. My speed was much too fast on the approach, and when my accessory-free bike took to the air there was no turning back. I quickly descended to the bottom of the gulch, briefly disappearing from view. I was then jettisoned up on the other side, flipping completely over and landing sideways with what I thought might be my last hurrah. Shaken up, I gathered myself, tended to my skinned knees and elbows, picked up my bike, adjusted the handlebars and looked around, hoping someone had witnessed this feat. To my dismay there was no one around. Without further delay I remounted and returned to join my buddies as if nothing had happened. I was forever left to remember my epic flight all to myself.

At one time or another all of us kids jumped curbs, bailed off our bikes at break-neck speeds and flew across ditches and neighborhood creeks, continually defying the odds. BMX and Motorcross had yet to be invented. I guess we were pioneers and didn't know it.

Safety measures were of little concern. Throwing caution to the wind, we often rode with the no-hands method just to show off. No one wore a helmet. Our summertime attire usually included a pair of old Red Ball Jets, Red Goose or Chuck Taylor Converse tennis shoes, and maybe a t-shirt (if that) and a pair of shorts (no cut-off jeans in those days). Socks were optional as were the shoes. Other apparel consisted of a pair of Lee Dungarees or Levi blue jeans (no arm or shin guards and no gaudy Tour-de-France attire).

One precaution we always adhered to, however, was rolling up the right pant leg. This prevented the chain from grabbing a portion of our trousers, which would cause the bike and the rider to encounter a sudden halt, resulting in a disastrous crash. Doubling someone on the back fender required kids to roll up both pant legs to avoid the spokes. Riding on the handlebars was treacherous but that did not deter us. The only safety precaution we took seriously was car avoidance.

Lighter European machines eventually entered the scene, enabling a long ride to be made more comfortably. I had a Raleigh three-speed that, to me, was a revolution. I could go up a hill without having to stand up and pedal. We used to think it was cool to coast down a hill and crank the pedals backwards. The sound the chain made was easily recognizable. We even had front and rear brakes that were controlled by your hands. My friend, John Williams, used his 10-speed 1963 Western Flyer to circle the city with fellow classmates in 1965 (see news article in the January 2010 issue of The Nashville Retrospect).

Age 16 and the eligibility to drive a car ended our cycling days. Looking back, the camaraderie with friends, the conversations passed between us while cruising neighborhood streets, and the great adventures we shared riding bikes made my early years some of the best times of my life.

CHAPTER 5

Hair's the Story

BACK IN 1954 there were over 180 barbershops in our city. Eight chairs or more were not uncommon. Most all of the hotels had one. The Noel, The Sam Davis, Hermitage, Andrew Jackson and the Maxwell House were a few. There was one at Union Station, the Melrose building, Stahlman Building, and at the Arcade, called the Annex Barber Shop. The Doctor's Building Barber Shop, Stahlman Building Barber Shop, Sudekum Building Barber Shop, and the Third National Bank Building Barber Shop all were located in those facilities' basements. Sanitary Barber Shop had several locations. The Elks Club had one and so did the Y on 4th Avenue North. There was one in the basement of the May Hosiery Mill on Chestnunt Street, and for those west of town, the Logan Center Barber Shop was on Highway 100.

The Hippodrome Roller Rink on West End Avenue had a shop next to it at 2621 called Hippodrome Barber Shop, operated by Joe W. Jones, C.E. Mills and Obadiah D. Freeman. They were black barbers in the white part of town, unusual for that time period. My neighbor Alex accompanied his father on occasion, as that was his dad's barber.

Keep in mind there were just as many beauty shops as barbershops. Every department store offered hair care for the ladies while many places catered to both men and women, especially the hotels. The Bon-Ton in the Hillsboro Village area had both services, as did the Arcade section of downtown. Every part of town cut hair. Throughout the 1950s, 1960s and into the 1970s the industry thrived.

There comes a time when parents give up the hair cutting process and turn it over to the local barber or beautician. For me it occurred sometime around my seventh or eighth birthday, probably during the year of 1954. The

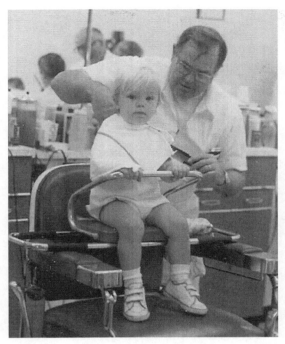

Barber Ralph Dishman works with a young client circa 1980 at Belle Meade Barber Shop.

red-white-and-blue pole twirling around out front was carnival-like and lessened the apprehension of the new adventure.

Fortunately, at that time I was not privy to the history of the barber pole, which was originally a symbol of bloodletting procedures done by barbers who cut more than hair in the Middle Ages. A shaft was used for the customers to grip, which accentuated their bluing veins so that knives and leeches could be applied. A bowl housing those leeches was part of the paraphernalia and was used to catch the blood. Yikes. After the procedure, bandages would be applied and later hung around the shaft to dry, usually outside as an advertisement. As the wind blew the bloodied linens became wrapped around that shaft, creating a spiral effect. Hence the familiar barber pole that ended up symbolizing the local barbershop. A monthly hair cut and bloodletting would not have been part of my schedule.

My dad traveled frequently and was at work during the day, so it was initially my mother who took me to our local shop. The Harding Road Barber Shop (later called Belle Meade Barber Shop) actually had an address of 2 White Bridge Road. Owned by Tom Cooper, it was a convenient spot for moms because the Duchess Beauty Salon was right next door. Both kids and parents could get spruced up at the same time.

It was an unforgettable experience. Entering the door, next to the colorful pole on the outside wall, a jingle of bells would announce my arrival, followed by "Come in, young man," in an effort to give me that grown-up status. No matter how old I got the greeting was the same. If it was crowded we would take a number that was written on a circular tag and hung by a string over small hooks on a board attached to the wall, then sit down to wait facing the action. There were no appointments. It was a manly type place with hard, shiny floors and reading material strewn about. Boys Life, Highlights for Children, Field & Stream were just a few of them.

Posters like these were displayed in barbershops in the 1950s. Hair styling choices included Flat-Top Boogie, Executive Contour and Butch.

There were older men, all lathered up in various stages, sitting in leather chairs with other men hovering over them brandishing long blades and scraping off the foam in large quantities. There was a black fellow polishing shoes off to the side. In the window were a couple of high-school football schedules and carnival flyers facing to the outside. On the interior wall was a poster of the various hairstyles of the day: Flat tops, Crew Cuts, the Vanguard, Contour, etc. The Greaser and Duck Tail look was not there. Hoodlums, or "hoods" as we called them, mainly wore that style. I don't recall the price back then, but when David Strayhorn went he paid 75 cents.

When my number was called, a plank or booster seat was placed across the arms of the chair to prop me up to adult level. I stayed motionless while my mother would give instructions as the barber pushed down on a lever, thrusting the chair upward. All of those men wore white smocks as if surgery was about to take place. Fortunately, leeches were not involved. A large cape or sheet would be put over my chest. It was affixed around my neck with a separate small piece of tissue underneath to keep the small hairs from going

Blondes
... Ultra gives your hair glint and sparkle.

Brunettes
... Ultra brings out those glisteam highlights.

For every shade of hair

Redheads
... Ultra adds depth and glowing colour.

Ultra Loveliness

ultra

As Ultra Home Perm brings new beauty to your hair. Set your hair into any one of dozens of smart different hair-dos made possible by Ultra's soft, long-lasting, easy-to-place curls. You—and others—will see how attractive and becoming your hair really is.

SUCCESS GUARANTEED!
The full Ultra Home Perm Kit contains Creme Waving Lotion, Rubber Bands, End papers — Processing Cap (only Ultra gives this), 60 Special Easy-wind Plastic Curlers —everything to give yourself a lovelier permanent wave ... and only Ultra gives you the essential, thorough, Liquid Neutraliser, and an absolute MONEY-BACK GUARANTEE of success.

The gentle **ultra**
Home Permanent
with Liquid Neutraliser

An ad from the 1950s touts home permanent products for women.

into my shirt. The process would begin with the "snip, snip" of scissors shortening my hair with the aid of a comb.

Those combs, along with scissors, blades and other objects of the trade, would be kept in a tall jar of blue sanitizing liquid that said Barbicide on it and sat in front of a huge mirror on the back bar, along with all sorts of tonics and other items. There was Pinaud Clubman After Shave, Wildroot Crème Oil, Butch Wax, Murray's pomade in small tins, Bay Rum (not for drinking...usually), Lilac Vegetal, the familiar red or blue bottle of Lucky Tiger hair tonic, some Old Spice and others.

The Flat Top was a favorite, as most kids wanted the Ricky Nelson and later Johnny Unitas type of look. This haircut basically was a burring of the head with the front being left a little longer. It was just a tuft of hair but when Butch Wax was applied it would stand straight up. At room temperature the wax would stiffen, so a brief, two-block walk during the winter often caused freezing. It was flammable as well. A spark from a fireplace could turn your head into a torch. Great stuff, that Butch Wax.

After the scissoring ended, the electric shears came out, trimming my sideburns and sprucing up the back of my neck. I thought that was it until the heavy-duty ones surfaced. The sound they made was a lower hum than the regular clippers. When they were placed behind the ears for the close finishing touch, your entire head would vibrate. My friend Paul happened to have an earache one day and let out a blood-curdling scream when it was used on

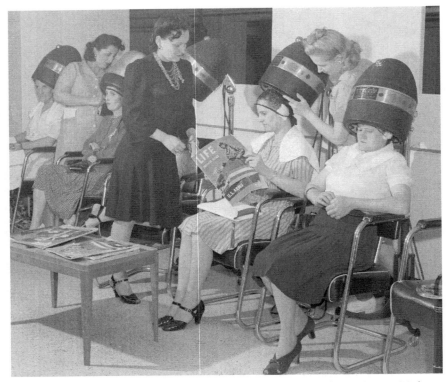

Women have their hair styled and dried in a department store beauty shop in Detroit, Mich., in 1941. (Library of Congress)

him, startling not only his mom but also the entire shop. When the final buzzing ended, a splashing of back-bar tonics and a brief massage of my scalp took place, followed by a combing and parting of what was left of my mane.

The cape and tissue were then removed. One more step to go. The soft bristles of a handheld brush, saturated with a talc of some kind, were used to whisk away any remnants of my hair. I became engulfed in a cloud of white fragrance. A quick whirl around to look in the mirror to view the masterpiece and back again to seek a favorable response from my mother, then a lowering of the leather chair, and I was done.

There was no cashier. After getting paid and receiving a tip, the barber himself did the honor of pulling the lever on the cash register, making a "ka-ching" sound. I dropped a penny in the gumball machine by the entrance and was ushered out the door by the pleasant "Y'all come back to see us." The clean, fresh smell seemed to last for days; it was an invigorating experience.

Girls would often go with their moms to salons or to department stores to get prettied up and pampered. Carolyn (Selph) Henderson remembers a trip to Roy Carter's at 2512 Franklin Road with her mom. On one occasion Mr. Carter took her up in his small airplane for a spin and flew right over her house on Draughon Avenue. To a 7- or 8-year-old that was pretty cool. Now that was extra pampering.

For the lassies it was all about curls, waves and volume. Some gals did their permanents at home, at least in my family's case. With a mother and two sisters in the house, I regularly was subjected to noxious fumes of ammonia seemingly in a stagnant state throughout our residence.

Home permanents were the thing. I remember seeing Toni, Lilt and Quick boxes strewn about. Toni had a 15-minute show on television in 1950 with twins fixing each other's hair. All the men tuned in for that. These "systems" were applied to rolled hair and allowed to sit for hours to aid in the curling process. The time sitting under a tall steel pole with a helmet circulating hot air around the head occupied most of their day. The good thing was I could make derogatory comments about them and they would never know because they couldn't hear. But my watering eyes and me usually vacated the premises during this entire procedure.

By the late '50s portable dryers were popular. Women could walk around the house, do chores or lie in the bed and read, as long as a plug was nearby. General Electric's Deluxe Hair Dryer and the 1965 Lady Sunbeam Jet Set became the new thing in the bonnet style. Those rigid, alien-looking contraptions were mainly relegated to local beauty salons.

Ralph Dishman worked for Tom Cooper at Harding Road Barber Shop beginning in 1960. When Cooper retired he took over and stayed there for 46 years. The name was eventually changed to Belle Meade Barber Shop. He had eight

The author's wife, Carolyn, uses a portable bonnet hair dryer in 1970.

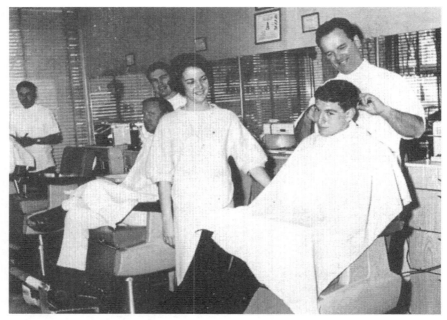

This photo of Oxford Barber Shop appeared in an ad in the 1967 Vanderbilt University annual. The author lived upstairs in the building the same year. (Dan Dahlinger)

chairs and occupied the No. 4 spot. Ralph recalls cutting one little 3-year-old's hair back in the late 1970s.

"I'll never forget him. He was the youngest of three that came in and the other two jumped into waiting chairs. He had to sit with his mother until a chair came open. I got him, and that little feller didn't move a muscle. Came back the next time and waited until he could go to my chair."

This gives you an idea of Ralph's expertise and service. After all, a local advertisement proclaimed, "Boys are our Specialty."

As far as female barbers went, Dishman said he "got calls about why I didn't hire no women. I told 'em I was full up, had no place to put 'em."

Good guys like Les, Shorty, Jim, Bill Stevens, Doug, Ralph and others clipped and shined folks up for decades there just as Denny Sitze and his family are now doing as they continue the tradition at the Belle Meade Barber Shop, located on Old Hickory Boulevard in Bellevue.

Austin and Young in the Wilson-Bates building next to Mallernee's Men's Store across from Hillsboro High was a regular for Hal Rosson in the late 1950s. While he was accustomed to being taken by his mom, the regular hair-cutting trip on one particular Saturday had his father at the wheel. Upon arriving he was asked by his pop which of the two barbers normally cut his hair. The clean-cut, well-groomed gentleman or the kind of scruffy-looking, shaggy-haired fellow. Young Rosson replied the "clean-cut guy." His dad responded by saying: "Today you are going to the scraggly-looking one. With only two barbers in this shop they obviously cut each other's hair. You can tell who gives the best hair cut." That shop's ad in the Hillsboro High football program of 1959 boasted they were the "Flat-Top Originators."

By the mid- to late 1960s, the number of shops stayed constant and were in most every hotel, large office building and commercial site.

Newlyweds in the fall of 1967, my wife and I lived in the Oxford House Apartments across from Peabody College (now part of Vandy) on 21st Avenue South. Ed Cole's Oxford Barber Shop was located on the first floor and had been since 1962, but as an enlisted man in the U.S. Army my hair was trimmed for free on a much too regular basis, so I had no use for the shop.

At my initial "trimming" at Fort Campbell as a new enlistee a year earlier, I was asked by their barber, "How would you like it?" Wanting to keep my longer golden locks without much damage I replied, "Take a little off the top and leave some sideburns." I was sheared back to crew cut status of 1954 within one minute. Evidently he misunderstood my instructions. At least I didn't get a Mohawk. I vowed to stay out of barbershops forever when my service days ended. I stayed true to

The author tended to avoid barbershops in the early '70s, having spent too much time in military barbershops in prior years.

that, much like many kids in the late 1960s and 1970s. I sported that long hair during my college days.

> *I almost cut my hair*
> *Happened just the other day*
> *It's getting' kind of long*
> *I could've said it was in my way*
> —Crosby, Stills, Nash and Young,
>   "Almost Cut My Hair" (1970)

The younger crowd generally began drifting away from the older barbershops as "hair styling" for men came into vogue in the 1970s. Sales of "A little Dab will do ya" Brylcreem and Vitalis "with V-7" greatly diminished. Our city directory in 1975 listed fewer than half of the number of shops that were in operation just 10 years earlier. Beauty shops maintained their appeal, and the older crowd continued the course for the men, but the demographics of the traditional shops shifted. They are still around, and barbers like 90-year-old Benjamin Flagg, who is still cutting away in his 60th year, are a testament to folks wanting that treatment of a bygone era.

Barbers back in my time were unknowing psychiatrists. They were good listeners and let you vent about whatever was bugging you. It was a man's place. The leather of the straps and chairs, soaps and shaving foam, shoe polish, talc, various oils, tonics and after-shaves all combined to give a pleasing distinctive aroma that remains to this day. Recalling those old pictures on the wall and the masculine banter you could hear over the humming of the razors in the background conjures up a certain nostalgia. It was one of the few spots where you could enter in a foul state and leave feeling and smelling like a new man. So if you can find one of those traditional shops, just tell the barber "take a little off the top and leave some side-burns." Maybe he will listen. If he does, be sure to tip and you just might hear him say, "Y'all come back to see us."

CHAPTER 6

Reflections on a Christmas Past

DISCOVERING SOMETHING for the first time can be good, bad or indifferent depending upon the find. Cleaning out a desk drawer of unwanted papers, pens, loose staples, rubber bands and the like, I happened upon an envelope inscribed with "Tom III." That was what I was called at family gatherings, for there would often be four Toms in the same room. It seemed to be empty until I ran my index finger inside and felt a square piece of cardboard. Extracting it I found it was an old Kodachrome slide, much larger than those taken by millions of folks in the 1960s and '70s. Written on the border was: "Tom III, Christmas 1947." And the slide was in color, no less.

Born the year before, on Dec. 3, 1946, I was just a needy, immobile, weeks-old baby on my first Christmas Day. So I gathered that this slide was the first picture of a Christmas scene where I appeared to be somewhat coherent.

The author with toys in a 1947 Christmas photo.

The author's sister Lynn holds the 1956 regional championship trophy. She was co-captain of the Hillsboro High School basketball team that year.

There I was sitting by the tree in the corner of our living room surrounded by bubbling ornaments, a metallic truck, a spinning top and a few blocks. That image set off a wave of sentiment, culminating in thoughts of my 10th holiday season—1956.

My sister Lynn had been very badly injured in an auto accident in the fall of 1953, wiping out her high-school basketball season and school as well. With the encouragement and aid of family, teachers, friends and the loving administrators at Hillsboro High, she eventually returned to the classroom and the hardwood where she excelled and was named co-captain of her 1956 team. I became a "mascot" of sorts for those girls. It was a crowning achievement and an emotional one for us all as she led her Burros to the regional championship one night in March. That was the pinnacle of girls basketball in those years. The song "Oh What A Nite" by the Dells released that same year was fitting.

The fear of nuclear weapons and communist invasions, our first test of an airborne hydrogen bomb over the island of Bikini Atoll, and Khrushchev bellowing "We will bury you!" all added excitement to a historic deluge of science-fiction movies. There was "Godzilla" and "Rodan," "Earth vs. the Flying Saucers" and "Plan 9 from Outer Space." I even bought a 45-rpm record entitled "The Flying Saucer" by Buchanan and Goodman, which was a novelty recording that hit No. 3 on the charts. "Forbidden Planet," featuring Robby the Robot, was one of the most popular sci-fi gems and spawned many remote-controlled robot toys. I got one that year and could program it by sliding levers in its back to make him go in certain directions. Any lever out of place would cause Robby to go nuts. I kind of enjoyed watching him go haywire.

As the Christmas season of 1956 approached, my mother went into another gear. I would often accompany her to shopping destinations and grocery outlets to stock up on holiday goodies. Cooper and Martin food store was a standard stop. They always had a deal for those housewives who used S&H Green Stamps. That year their newspaper advertisement enticed holiday gourmets with mouth-watering selections. A half-page ad in the Banner featured "Dubuque Sausage with Dried Skim Milk added in Vegetable Oil, 2 tins for only 25 cents." In that same edition, Sal Hepatica for constipation was offered (its tag line was "Take it and Smile"). Had mother bought the tins of sausage I feel sure the Sal Hepatica would not be needed. Mom always purchased a big turkey, ham and something called "spice round." That was a stomach turner to me. It looked like a ham but had white squares all through it. That and my dad's rhubarb pie seemed to grace our table throughout the holiday period. Both of those delicacies were safe in my presence.

Should one prefer dining out that holiday season, The Biltmore on Franklin Road at Craighead, and Bozeman's Restaurant at 438 Murfreesboro Road, both offered up chicken dinners for the low price of $1.35. Our family frequently dinned at Bozeman's, and it was a favorite of mine, for if I cleaned my plate the award was a toy truck. Can't get better than that.

If you smoked you could not miss those large festive ads for cigarettes such as Herbert Tareyton Filter and Cork Tips, Hit Parade, Pall Mall and Lucky Strike. We were non-smokers, at least I was until my teen years, and then it was on the sly.

The big shopping area was downtown Nashville. All the top department stores were located there as well as the big movie houses. It was a holiday must. Thousands of young girls lined up to see the new star, Elvis Presley, in his first motion picture "Love Me Tender" which had just opened in November, further enhancing the buying crowd. On Friday, Dec. 14, 1956, the Tennessee

The cover of the 1956 Sears Christmas catalog.

Marines hosted "Toys for Tots" at the Crescent Theater, and most of the other cinemas held cartoon specials on Saturdays for the sole purpose of collecting toys. Our town was good about that.

My taste in toys had changed from the spinning top, toy truck and blocks in 1947 to the "High and Low Bouncer" pogo stick (helmet not included) and more "mature" items that a 10-year-old would require. Ant farms and cowboy stuff was big. Harvey's sold a complete Roy Rogers outfit—including spurs, hat and pistols—for $4.98.

I used to love firing off that roll of caps and seeing the small vapor cloud appear after each trigger pull. The sulphur odor of those caps still resonates. Western Auto countered with a Wyatt Earp two-gun set for $4.95. Aladdin Industries manufactured Robin Hood, Hopalong Cassidy and cartoon lunch boxes for us to take our carefully-prepared sandwiches in for school. Those tin rectangles were big sellers that year. Most all of the stores had those rubbery one-inch army and cavalry soldiers and Indian figures that we used to pit against one another in battle. Sorry to say those Indians did not fare well in those days, at least in our eyes.

Cain-Sloan, Castner Knott and others had large toy sections displaying board games like Sergeant Preston and Forest Friends. The new game Yahtzee was introduced along with that sticky, clay-like substance hated by all parents called Play-Doh. There were portable phonographs, erector sets, and replicas of sports cars. Dinky Toys and Tonka ruled the day, cornering the miniature car, truck and bus scene.

The Sears catalog was the shopping bible of many. The Christmas cover created an anticipation rarely equaled by the contents. You could get anything from lingerie to lawn mowers within those hundreds of fully-illustrated pages. Found in the toy section that year were Happi-Time Pedal Sports Cars. Most cost just $13.88 while a real car was around $1,500. A child could fit into one of those miniatures and pedal away. There were wood-burning sets, English bikes and transistor radio kits. One such kit declared "It's an electronic wonder. Fun to assemble." Anything requiring assemblage was not fun for me. I was more of a Slinky-type action kid.

Christmas roller skating parties abounded, and I was often seen circling the polished wood at some of those held by classmates at Nashville's skate mecca, The Hippodrome. Friedman's, "On the Square," capitalized by selling

The original headline and caption from the Dec. 13, 1956, Nashville Banner: "The Hippodrome Is Scene Of Holiday Party—David Ferree, Clare Givan, Virginia Haley, Jean Wallace, Ellen Collins and Allen Patton entertained members of the school set at a recent skating party at The Hippodrome." (Nashville Public Library, Nashville Room, photo by Bob Ray)

A pedal car was used as an advertisement for West End Toyland. (Powell Phillips Jr.)

Powell Phillips poses in a pedal car at his store, Phillips Distributors, which was located at 8th Avenue South and Wedgewood. Today the store is Phillips Toy Mart located in Belle Meade. (Powell Phillips Jr.)

Chicago Shoe Skates for $11.98. I had my own, less-expensive, metal, clasps-over-the-loafer type. I was not a noted skate king.

You could order a live Christmas tree at Jones Ornamental Nursery on Hobbs Road for $5 by calling Cy (Cypress) 2-6383.

Competition was so fierce all the department stores had Santa come at one time or another. Harvey's advertised that you could get a photo sitting on Santa's lap for a dollar on their third floor with "no appointment needed." The big enticement was free Fleer's Dubble Bubble bubble gum to each child who visited him. The only time I remember doing that it was Santa who needed the gum, to quash his odorous breath.

Although downtown was the hot spot, a place called West End Toyland located at 30th and West End (next to Smiley's Restaurant and Candyland) started up about 1946, soon moving to 8th Avenue South and Wedgewood, where Powell Phillips changed the name to Phillips's Distributors. With WWII ending, Phillips started selling anything that would sell, from toys to fishing poles to heaters. The toys flew off the shelf, persuading the young entrepreneur to specialize. That toy mart became known as the best toy shop in the city, famous for having items you could not find anywhere else, with quality, I might add. It became an annual stop many Nashvillians considered a holiday ritual. I know we did. It was a good time to be a shopper.

At night at the Parthenon, we used to stop and just gaze at the Nativity Scene donated by Harvey's department store just two years earlier in 1954. It was a real spectacle and stretched over 280 feet with flashing, colorful lights brightening the skyline. A photograph appeared in the Nashville Banner on Dec. 3, 1956, on my 10th birthday, showing the crowd taking in that amazing display (see below). It left a lasting impression.

Original caption from a similar photo in the Dec. 3, 1956, Nashville Banner: "Babe and Mother rest beneath the shimmering star at the center. At the extreme right the first Wise Man may be seen approaching." (Nashville Public Library, The Nashville Room, photo by Paul Schleicher)

The author enjoys Christmas morning 1956 with this mother and two sisters. It was to be their last as a family living in the same house.

Christmas Day that year was as it had been, nothing really extraordinary: Candlelight service at West End Church on Christmas Eve, worship on Christmas Day, followed by the opening of gifts and the eating of great meals at home and at my grandparents'. Those meals were like a sacrament and the holy grail of eating to my mother—fine china, white tablecloth, once-a-year plates and glasses, the turkey on a silver platter ready for my dad to carve, cranberry ice in those tall parfait glasses, scalloped oysters and other delicacies, all placed strategically around our dining room table with seating pre-determined. I always sat to the left of my dad. We were to be well-dressed and properly mannered. The setting itself accentuated such. It made all of us be on our best behavior, at least for one day. It was similar to the dinners we had on Thanksgiving and all the Christmases that came before, not realizing at the time that it was a major milestone. I know now it was the last year that my immediate family would celebrate a Yuletide with all of us living in the same house, for the next year my oldest sister would marry and no longer live at home.

Those first 10 years were some of the best of my life, but in 1956 a sister had comeback from a horrific auto crash a few years earlier to win a basketball title for her school. Older sister was a well-respected collegian at Vandy as well as serving as a role model for us younger siblings, and Mom and Dad were happily married despite trying to cope with a young baby boomer such as me. It was a special Christmas all brought back to life by a long-forgotten Kodachrome slide .

The history and memories an old picture conjured up are irreplaceable. The messy contents of a particular desk drawer were, well...priceless.

CHAPTER 7

Learning to Dance

TORN SHIRT, muddy kneecaps, a pair of Red Ball Jets with shoestrings untied, dirt on my cheeks, a bike with baseball cards attached to the spokes, and a worn-out dog trailing behind—all could best describe me as a kid in the 1950s. The closest I had ever been to a dance floor was with my family at a dinner party when I was 3 years old. That was it. Once I hit the sixth grade my parents decided it was time I had some external refinement called "dance class." After all, both of my sisters were better off for it, so why shouldn't little brother benefit as well?

From the Depression era to the mid-1970s was the heyday of Junior High dance school. Unfortunately for me that was my era, too. Fletcher Harvey's Tweensters in Green Hills was my destination. This was where my indoctrination into the foxtrot occurred. I am sure Jeanette Noel wished I had never showed up. She was approximately six inches my superior and was just overall much larger. When pairing up to learn the familiar "box step" routine, my first move was to mash her large toe with my heel, having overstepped a bit. Amidst a muffled groan, my next move caused a knee-buckling reaction as both my feet came to rest upon hers. I figured a step up would increase my height considerably. She staggered, narrowly avoiding collapse. We did manage to finish out the routine but, as I recall, never touched again.

There were other such dance studios in Nashville during those years. Arthur Murray had a spot as did the Nick Lambos Academy of Dance run by Chris Lambos. Nicky, an energetic, fun-loving kid from Tennessee Industrial School, taught moves to folks for over 30 years, eventually marrying one of his students. Albertine Maxwell operated the Albertine School of Dance from 1936 to 1980, teaching ballet to thousands of youngsters in her studio at

An accomplished student demonstrates a dance step to the other students circa 1940 at Fortnightly dance studio. (Ann Fort)

her home at 3325 West End Ave. A historical marker states she was regarded as the symbol of dance in her adopted hometown of Nashville. The name Albertine's still resonates with the dance community to this day.

Another name synonymous with instruction into adolescent dance techniques was Fortnightly. It was launched in 1935 by famed artist Cornelius Hankins' daughter, Eleanor Hankins. She married Walter Fort and went by the name of Hank. After teaching kids to tap dance at Parmer Elementary School and showcasing them at the Belle Meade Theatre's Happiness Club, she decided to open a comparable learning facility for 11-, 12- and 13-year-olds. She called it Fortnightly using the name of a popular, exclusive club in Chicago she had researched. After Hank teamed up with an astute and stern business partner, Mrs. Martha Perkins Trousdale, and later Carol Woolwine, Hank Fort's Fortnightly Club was off the ground.

It initially met in country clubs, Parmer School, a home and even the Oriental Club before coming to terms with the famous Albertine Maxwell to use her fine house on West End.

Limited to 30 students initially, it only met on Saturdays but advanced to Thursdays, Fridays and Saturdays with two sessions each. An annual costume party held at the old Centennial Club on 8th Avenue for all the pupils was the highlight of the year during that time and was the talk of the town.

Hank became so popular with her talent and personality that she eventually relocated to Washington, D.C., to entertain the hierarchy in 1952. She recorded records, appeared on the Arthur Godfrey and John Q. Lewis television shows and performed at the Copa, among other things.

She divorced and remarried in 1949 but continued to commute back and forth just so she could teach at her Fortnightly Club.

One song, "Look with Pride on our Flag," was dedicated to Richard Nixon and was performed at his inauguration, while "Cherry Blossom Spring" was played at the 1972 Cherry Blossom Festival in Washington. Her "Put Your Shoes on Lucy" became a national favorite. Hank was even called to entertain President Lyndon Johnson and wife, Ladybird, in Texas. Her niece-in-law, Ann Fort, said she was a master hostess.

The entrance to Albertine's home was fronted by several long ascending steps. Both sexes would sit there prior to class but usually the boys would wait until the last minute, often summoned in with a "Come on in boys—time to start" from Mrs. Trousdale. A walk up into the foyer, where innocent

A photo from the 1960s shows Hank Fort (center) instructing sixth-graders Louie Buntin and Anne Thomas while Mary Pirtle and Allen Cargile Jr. observe. (Ann Fort)

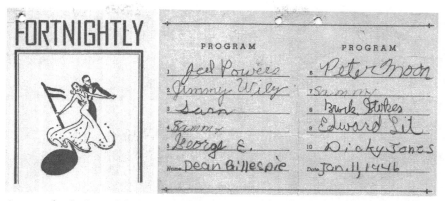

An example of a Fortnightly dance card (front and inside), which had to be filled with names of dance partners. This one belongs to Dean Gillespie and dates to January 1946

mingling occurred, and a turn to the right would put the kids into the open ballroom with huge mirrors and ballet rails. This is where the instruction took place.

Each child was expected to be finely dressed—coats, ties, white shirts, and polished shoes for the boys, while the girls had much more to assemble. Through the years, hair ribbons, evening dresses, long white gloves (to conceal sweating), cumbersome girdles, garters, nylon panty hose, crinolines and the like, along with appropriate makeup, were part of the attire.

Aside from ballroom dancing, the youngsters were instilled with an appreciation of proper etiquette, stately manners, and how to act like gentlemen and ladies. I suppose that was the main reason for a good number of participants taking the class. Dean Gillespie attended in the early 1940s and was a ballet student under Albertine as well. She said manners in those early years were not emphasized, for, as she put it, "We were all mannerly back then; we knew how to act."

Class began with all the pupils in a circle amid opening remarks by Hank, often in her tight, animal-skin dress and sometimes tapping her cane on the floor to grab attention. Next up was a demonstration of the evening steps to be learned. Children would watch the expert and try to mimic moves while in place, then eventually move to the music with a partner, all as Mrs. Trousdale put on the record. In the late 1950s and early 1960s, music by Frankie Avalon, Chuck Berry, the Big Bopper, Chubby Checker and the Coasters blasted over radios. But at 3325 West End Avenue, Johann Strauss and Tchaikovsky ruled supreme. Instead of "Yakety Yak" or "Sweet Little 16," everyone tried to float about the polished floor to "Blue Danube," "Swan Lake" and "Waltz of the Flowers." The Fly, Twist and Mashed Potato were out; the waltz, foxtrot, two-step, tango and cha-cha were in. It was a real shock to the system.

This prize bracelet was won by Carolyn (Selph) Henderson with Roger DeSilvestro in a 1959 waltz contest.

Small dance cards were issued to both sexes with orders to fill them out by having your selection personally sign each one. This was no problem for some, but for others it was a nightmare. There were ten spots to have autographed. Judy (Hinton) Oliver sat with the other girls with their dance cards as the boys came by to fill them up.

"There was jockeying among both to get someone good on your card," said Oliver, "and avoid the geeks as much as possible."

As each dance ensued one was to find his or her mate for that particular number and proceed to join others on the floor as Hank watched and weaved among them, offering advice and constructive criticism. In an article by Millie Milam Murphy, one young boy asked Hank about breaking in: "Miss Fort, when you see a girl you want to dance with, how do you get rid of the one you got?" The answer was not given.

Oddly enough, many a young man enjoyed the experience. Stokes Elementary's Hal Rosson was one; he said his father would sing "Put Your Shoes On Lucy" before every session and seemed to enjoy the prodding of his son. On the other hand, Alex Slabosky from Woodmont School said it was one of the worst experiences of his life.

Another Stokes attendee in 1945, Nancy Holt Garvey, did not have the time of her life, she says because she was fat and the tallest one in the class. Her incomplete dance card has not been framed nor has the Mother Goose costume she wore at the costume party. Stokes had a number of kids in regular attendance providing a comfort zone for fellow classmates. One of those, Carolyn (Selph) Henderson, won the waltz contest with Roger DiSilvestro in 1959 and was awarded a bronzed leaf and pearl bracelet (see photo above).

Rosson said his mother wanted him to go to improve his less-than-desirable manners. His parents drove the "hookup" on Fridays. Like most testosterone-laden boys, he decided to impress the girls with his first ever slathering of English Leather cologne all over his wool suit. Must have been a choking experience for Sam Weedman, Allen Reed and others in the car.

This was not unlike the experience of Maggie Griffin Dunne who was suffocated by the smell of Brut as the only female to ride in her car. John Claybrook said he used "a splash of Hai Karate, and I was ready to go!"

The girls also applied cologne and perfume in eye-watering amounts. Anne Clayton put on "as much Yardley make-up as we could get away with."

Jim Leinart attended in 1962 and "stepped on a lot of toes and feet" and still does, he said.

Linda (Alford) Scott, a '57 alum, will never forget going upstairs to take off her Mouton coat and white gloves and being chased by Albertine's German Shepard. It was quite frightening. The smell of kitty litter was also not forgotten by Patricia Rees Roblin.

Whether you liked going or not, the normal bribe by parents was an after-class trip downtown to the Sweet Shop, Candyland for the Chocolate Drifts, across the street to Krispy Kreme Donuts or a ride to Blankenship Drugs for a soda.

Although most kids during the first few decades were well-behaved and learned quickly, some needed a little more tutoring, especially on their dance steps. In 1959, Woodmonters Paul Clements and Cathy Hamilton supposedly lost control during a foxtrotting Mexican Hat Dance routine and careened into several couples, causing a small pile-up of young bodies, panty hose, dinner jackets and white gloves. I am sure Mrs. Trousdale felt there was no intent in the missteps, but I believe otherwise. Clements attended on Saturdays and often disappeared into the cloak room to listen as Larry Munson broadcast

This photo of a Fortnightly costumed dance appeared in the Dec. 17, 1965, Nashville Banner captioned: "The Academy Award motion picture, 'Separate Tables,' sever as inspiration for costumes worn by Julie Davidson and Craige DeMoss Jr., left and right, to the 1959 costume party for eighth graders. Seen in the center are Scott Harris and Kathi Woods." (Ann Fort)

Vandy basketball games. A student of Hank's in the early 1940s and eventual instructor while Hank was away, Myrtle Ann Archer, recalls one grade school class from Ensworth being particularly unmannerly. Mrs. Trousdale was horrified and decided to call a special meeting of the entire group's parents to address the situation. Unfortunately only the parents of the kids that were well-behaved showed up. Par for the course, I guess.

Mrs. Archer taught from the late 1960s into the 1970s. She stressed etiquette and courtesy, continuing the tradition set by her predecessor.

"The main things we taught were the waltz, foxtrot, samba and tango," she said, "but I was really dead set on the manners. Along with the dancing, you gave your name when addressed and especially to older folks."

Kids would hold out their hand and say, "Good evening, Mrs. Archer"—just like they used to say to Hank when leaving: "Goodnight, Mrs. Fort." Some mischievous pupils would subtly replace the "o" with an "a." You get the picture.

For instruction, Myrtle used the same tried-and-tested format, especially during the waltz contests. She and her assistants, sisters Carol Woolwine and

Maggie Trousdale, would play the music, walk amongst the couples and tap each contestant on the shoulder indicating who would remain waltzing when the music concluded. The final couple standing was the winner. Applause and cheers would erupt for the winning duo. Archer said all the kids were "dressed to kill" and looked so nice, but when asked if that made their deportment exemplary, she replied with a laugh: "Not so sure about that."

A few of those who lacked in certain areas would be privately tutored at her home on Paddock Place. She, like Hank, genuinely cared for each child.

Hank Fort died Jan. 12, 1973, and the home of Albertine Maxwell no longer exists. Fortnightly continued on in other locations with dedicated instructors. The dance clubs of those times have since disappeared. The thousands of 11-, 12- and 13-year-olds who attended were shown how to be gentlemen and ladies, to be courteous and kind to others, and to gracefully sashay across a ballroom floor to time-honored classics. It worked for most boys and girls as we got older, others not so much. One thing for sure, we were all better off for it.

> *Put your shoes on Lucy*
> *Even though they kinda pinch*
> *Stop that balking,*
> *You're going to do some walking,*
> *It's a cinch*
> *Use your party manners,*
> *You'll need them and how*
> *Put your shoes on Lucy,*
> *You're a big girl now.*
> —Hank Fort, "Put Your Shoes on Lucy" (1949)

CHAPTER 8

Doing the Laundry

COMING ACROSS an old Columbus washboard conjured up a memory of my childhood that had been forgotten over the years. You see, washing clothes from the '40s through the '60s was quite the chore for women everywhere. For my mother, having a husband and two daughters to clean for was no easy task, but when I came along some eight years after my youngest sister, it amplified the whole procedure. I kept Mom extremely busy

The author's sisters—Beth, age 6, and Lynn, age 4— play in a washtub in 1942.

with grass-stained knees, elbows and dirty undergarments. I alone soiled enough clothes for three kids.

Doing the laundry for us all started underground. We had a full basement in our home much like all homes built in those days. They were mainly constructed that way to provide space for the large coal furnaces that provided homes with heat. To get to our basement required entering through the breakfast room and carefully descending numerous wooden steps. To a little kid it was a place of mystery, with stuff hanging from the rafters and sitting on back shelves here and there. Mother had a white, slate-looking table down

At left, a woman uses a washboard and two washtubs to clean clothes in 1938. At right is the brass-and-wood washboard used by the author's mother for many decades. (Library of Congress)

there that always had garments laid out on it. Against the foundation wall were two large metal sinks built as one piece with a faucet in the middle and a large black hose under the bottom that went to the floor for drainage to a hole some five feet away.

I believe these were installed after my appearance, for what I remember most about those bins was a place to bathe our four-legged pets.

There was a machine next to the table called a "wringer" as I recall. It looked like a rolling pin attached to a crank perched atop a large tank. The old Maid-Rite washboard of ours was almost passé by the mid-1950s but was a necessity for my mother before that, and was usually on the table or in one of those two sinks. I rarely saw that wringer in action or much scrubbing of clothes on the brass-and-wood washboard because I was too young.

What I did see used was a large galvanized tub with handles that I played in outside during the hot summer months. Fill that thing with water and, voilá, an instant swimming hole. A picture of my sisters in that receptacle in our back yard in 1942 and me several years later showed its versatility. Its main use was for holding cleaning solution and for soaking and scrubbing clothes on the washboard.

Detergent companies competed for the approval of housewives like there was no tomorrow, especially in the late '50s and '60s. Mother used a variety of those products. I explicitly remember an old container of Oakite ("The Modern Detergent") sitting off to the side and the familiar box of Ivory Snow as well. Something called Rinso ("with sodium") was on a shelf, although I thought it was a mouse or pest control product of some kind. There were multitudes of those products, many of which I recall made an appearance in our home. To name a few, there was Lux, All, Dreft, Fab, Ivory Flakes, Oxydol, and Niagra Laundry Starch (to stiffen our finer shirts, I am sure, for special occasions—the collars usually chaffed my neck). There was Dash, Wisk, Surf, Daz, Cheer and Tide. Cheer and Tide were the most prevalent in our home. Competition for business was so fierce for the woman of the house that promotions included dishes and towels that came inside the actual containers. I know Duz, Gain and Bonus had dishes and a detergent called Breeze had towels. If you were a savvy buyer I guess you could accumulate enough dishes to stock a china cabinet. All of these washing powders and flakes my mother used had a scent that floated up from our basement and created pleasing odors that, for whatever reason, were comforting.

In addition to the cleaning solutions and powders, washing and drying machine manufacturers accelerated their efforts, especially in the '50s when television advertising reached millions of viewers. The newer washers had a built-in spinner to help dissipate the water, eliminating the need for the wringers.

Electric dryers, in some circles, were marketed by stating that the time saved from hanging clothes on a line gave the housewife more freedom to do other chores. That must have been exciting to the ladies. They were pricey, and when they did become affordable we still continued for years to hang all of our belongings on a clothesline located outside the kitchen door, down some steps and into the side yard. They were brought there, in my infant years, after being put through the wringer in the basement by way of a large, wicker clothes basket.

The actual washing of clothes occurred most frequently on a Monday. I am guessing because husbands had returned to work and kids went back to school, giving the lady of the house freedom to get all her chores done without interruption. On weekends in the fall, we would burn leaves (see Chapter

A clothesline is pictured on a farm in Morgan county in the 1930s. (Tennessee State Library and Archives)

23), an activity that was not a friend of clean clothes hanging on the line.

Some families had the "umbrella" clothesline. It was a contraption with multiple appendages attached to a single pole in the center and resembling an umbrella. More clothes could be put out to dry, but the clothes placed in the center seemed to take longer to dry. Carolyn (Selph) Henderson said they used one in their backyard on Draughon Avenue. In our case, two plastic lines were attached to two steel poles that looked liked a seven-foot-tall "T." Each one was wrapped and tied on the straight part of the crossbar of the "T" and stretched to the other one some 30 or 40 feet away. There were also devices you could buy that contained a retractable line. These usually were attached to wooden poles or bolted on in some fashion. We were not that sophisticated.

There was a procedure and method to Mother's hanging of the garments. First, the line had to be wiped with a wet cloth to remove residue of dust, bird mess and the like before any item was hung. Clothes were affixed with wooden, spring-action clothespins that were easy to squeeze open and apply. Before these pins came along she used the larger wooden variety that slid down over the item as it lay over the line. There was a separate small bag filled with these pins she usually carried out with her.

My mother was so proficient she could hang all of our clothes and all of the linen items up at one time without having to make two different trips. It was amazing. There was a method to this madness. She didn't just pin our stuff "willy-nilly." To minimize clothespin use one pin could hold part of two items. Our socks were hung by the toes, shirts by their tails and britches by the pant leg and not the waist. Dainties and unmentionables were usually on the back line so as not to be visible. It helped that we had a tall hedgerow blocking direct view from the neighbors. Nosy folks could tell what everyone wore by just examining the clothesline. I really wasn't interested in what type of underwear some of our neighbors, like the Ritters, the Sumpters or the Slabosky family, hoisted over their private areas every morning.

After all were hung a long rod was pushed up in the middle of the line to create several feet of space so that the sheets

This Super Suds ad appeared in the April 1, 1954, Nashville Banner. (Tennessee State Library and Archives)

and weight of the wet items would not drag the ground or come in contact with neighborhood dogs that ran freely in those days. Mother Nature then took over. The breeze and sun would do the trick.

Winter was no deterrent to hanging out clothes if the sun was out, for freezing clothes dried too and had that added moisture to them when the ironing process took place. On rainy days or if a sudden shower erupted my mother (and my sisters before me) would make a quick dash out to the line for removal. A subsequent re-attachment to a line we had in our basement was the standby.

After the clothes were dried, my mother would un-pin them from the line, place them in the basket and bring back into the house, whereupon the long task of ironing took place. The only thing I will say about this is that she used an empty Pepsi or Royal Crown Cola bottle filled with water and corked with a stopper of some kind that she had poked small holes in. She used this to sprinkle over the clothes before applying the hot iron. I thought it was neat. After that, the clothes were folded and put away.

I will say this, if as a child you never slept on air-dried sheets you have missed one of life's pleasures. The feel and fresh smell as you covered up is an unforgettable childhood memory.

Many TV commercials often pictured a smiling homemaker standing next to blowing clothes on a bright, sunny, windy day. You would never know all the hard work that went into getting to that stage. There really were no hazards to drying clothes in this manner other than from the occasional robin or cardinal droppings or from youngsters like me who played out at night and gallivanted through friends' yards. You had to watch out because a real "clotheslining" could take place if you were not observant; those poles were unforgiving—I know firsthand. We also liked to run between the bedspreads and sheets as they flapped in the wind. That was only a hazard if you got caught. I suspect my mother knew.

Time moved on and eventually clotheslines disappeared. Some cities and states even banned the practice, saying clotheslines were unsightly and indicative of poorer neighborhoods. Homeowner associations outlawed them as well, saying they were blemishes to their community. Our clothesline remained in place for decades. Mother hung clothes on lines as a child, as a newlywed bride and all the way to grandmother status, even though she had the dryer.

Technology and progress have made the backyard clothesline a thing of the past. If she were here today the following sentiments by a grandmother, Sheila Parks, would be approved: "From the time I had to tip-toe to reach the lines, I found it one chore I'd rather be doing than washing dishes or sweeping. It meant a few precious moments to be alone. As I became a teenager it gave me time to dream of all the tomorrows in my life. When I was a young bride, I found myself standing there smiling at the future with the man of my

This Sterchi's advertisement appeared in the May 18, 1950, Nashville Banner. Some of the featured items are: full length clothes line, galvanized rinse tub and "88 other useful pieces." (Tennessee State Library and Archives)

dreams. With a family of my own, I often used the time to figure out budgets, plan meals or just let my mind drift with the clouds above. Now I'm a grandmother with a much smaller load, but nowhere to hang them! After all, I could still use some sunshine on my soul and clothespins in my pocket!"

The hanging of clothes did not take place just in our side yard but in every back yard in all the neighborhoods in town. It was a part of the landscape back then. Should the wind blow just right one could get a whiff of that clean, fresh smell from the neighbor's clothes as well. It was another piece of Americana now moving farther away from us. For me, I think I will go put up a line.

CHAPTER 9

Hot Rods

We had twin pipes and a Columbia butt,
You people may think that I'm in a rut,
But to you folks who don't dig the jive,
That's two carburetors and an overdrive.
—Arkie Shibley and The Mountain Dew Boys,
  "Hot Rod Race" (1950)

MEN COMING home from World War II had a lot of time on their hands and some skill in metal working acquired by driving and tinkering with machines during their time in the service. In the dry lakes and salt flats of Southern California, between the towns of Burbank, Pasadena and Glendale, shade-tree mechanics built "hot rod" cars and raced them on the wide-open spaces. Model A and Model T Fords were cheap, readily available and lightweight. They were souped-up with no tops, only one seat and no ornaments or fenders. They were designed for speed.

The hot-rod craze took off in the late 1940s and 1950s with kids flocking to watch drag races. In 1947 Hot Rod magazine began promoting a do-it-yourself mentality. Having only one car, most young men drove their machines to the race sites, engaging in street duals along the way. These unauthorized competitions became popular. With the advent of television, rock 'n' roll and movies adding to the trend, these "hot rodders" were perceived as a trouble-making generation of juvenile delinquents. Foremost was James Dean, a film star and a juvenile cult figure idolized by teens and disliked by adults. His movie roles personified the troubled youth of that period. To diffuse this negativity, organizations such as the NHRA (National Hot Rod

Actor Broderick Crawford poses for a publicity photo for the television show "Highway Patrol."
He starred as Chief Dan Mathews on the show from 1955 to 1959.

Association) came on the scene emphasizing the positive qualities of engineering, craftsmanship and safety, to little avail.

As those wartime kids starting driving in the early 1950s, the younger baby boomers got a full dose of what was a newfound freedom. Songs about fast cars, racing and the like got my attention.

The tune that started it all was "Hot Rod Race," recorded in 1950 by a country group called Arkie Shibley and The Mountain Dew Boys. It introduced automobile racing to the youth of the day and into the culture. It inspired the follow up "Hot Rod Lincoln" by Charlie Ryan, and later in 1960 by Commander Cody and the Lost Planet Airmen. Chuck Berry's hit "Maybelline" in 1955 and "Beep Beep" by The Playmates in 1958 followed those up.

By the time I was 14, I bought an instrumental album by The Duals featuring the song "Stick Shift." The song was so popular the boys appeared on "American Bandstand" on Oct. 3, 1961. I played it over and over, mostly at 78 rpms rather than the normal 33 1/3. I realized if you sped up the sound of rubber being laid by the car in the background, it would really sound cool. My friends and I loved it. I liked the instrumentals and picked up the 45 record of the Frogmen strumming away at "Underwater." Like The Duals they also were on "American Bandstand," in April 1961. The Jimmy Gilmer and his Fireballs hit of 1959 entitled "Torquay" ended up in my collection as well. These instrumentals were deemed car songs and actually were the precursors to surf music that was soon to come.

Movies like "Thunder Road" with Robert Mitchum in 1958 further popularized the craze. It was a tale about running moonshine in Tennessee and Kentucky in the back of a souped-up 1951 Ford two-door. The movie theme song, "Ballad of Thunder Road," became a big hit.

On television we watched "Highway Patrol" featuring the portly, fedora-wearing Broderick Crawford in his 1955 Buick Century patrolling two-lane highways, even though he did not go fast enough for some of us.

Hot-rod flicks were not as refined as "Highway Patrol." Mostly of the B variety, they appeared at the Knickerbocker and 5th Avenue theaters downtown and later all of them became hits at the drive-ins. Such classics as "Hot Rod Gang," "Hot Rod Rumble," "Hot-Rod Girl" and "Ghost of Dragstrip

The original poster for the 1956 movie "Hot-Rod Girl."

Hollow" graced the screens in the 1950s. "Hot Rods to Hell" of 1967 had critics saying the movie was so bad it was actually entertaining. The mid-1960s fared better movie-wise for autos. "Bullitt" in 1968, which starred Steve McQueen blistering the pavement of San Francisco with his '68 Mustang GT 390, was arguably the best of the genre.

Most every kid knew someone who had a hot ride. Dick Jewel said he wasn't fortunate enough to have such a machine in high school. His 1953 lime-green, Moon discs, mainline Ford six-cylinder, with no radio or air conditioning, had to suffice. His brother Johnny had an old black Dodge affectionately named "BT" for "black turd." The redeeming quality: a huge back seat which saw frequent activity. Harry Guffee was always seen around Williamson County in a red '59 Chevy convertible, a Jeep and a '57 Ford hardtop convertible, while Gary Anderson's 1956 Chevy with two four-barrel carburetors got stolen. Poor boy had to then drive a push-button Dodge.

A 1964 advertisement for the Oldsmobile 4-4-2.

In 1963, when I was a junior in high school and into my driving years, John Delorean at Pontiac, along with others, slipped a 389-cubic-inch engine into a new 1964 Tempest Coupe, making it arguably the first "muscle car." They named it Gran Torismo Omologato (a phrase that originates with Italian cars and roughly means "approved for official long-distance races"). The famous GTO was born. Teens labeled it The Great One. Local Hillsboro High singing group Ronnie and the Daytonas capitalized

The author poses beside his then-new 1967 Chevrolet Camaro SS along with Moises Dias, a Vanderbilt exchange student staying with the Henderson family at the time.

on the car's popularity with their 1964 recording "Little G.T.O." I never had one but friends did. They were sweet.

Big engines became the thing for kids. There were 409s and 427s. There were even 4-4-2s put out by Oldsmobile, but the number wasn't the cubic inches of the engine. It featured a four-barrel carburetor, a four-speed manual transmission, and dual exhaust pipes.

Plymouth later came with the Barracuda and Roadrunner, and recording greats Jan and Dean, The Beach Boys, The Rip Chords and others immortalized some of those rides with national hits. One friend had a black 1962 Impala 409 with red interior and made the mistake of racing down Franklin's main street with none other than the governor's nephew. Their penance involved manually placing highway safety stickers in all the schools (a lot of good that did). They should have ventured to the Union Hill Drag strip or entered the Hobby Races at the Fairground Speedway.

Not surprisingly, teens who had the means got the nice rides. Jere Carter and Dan Fleming both had 427 Corvettes. But a lot of us drove what we were allowed to drive. After "collecting" five speeding violations during my last two years in high school, I was fortunate to drive the family's blue Chevrolet station wagon. Removing the air filter gave it that whirring noise, often

The author's sister Beth is pictured at Rice University in 1954 with a jalopy in the background.

attracting local authorities.

Ed Graham had a black 1957 Ford Fairlane. He converted the column shift to a four-on-the-floor with a customized gear knob, a big deal back then. Those knobs became fashion statements and so highly desired they were often pilfered. We spent a lot of time driving around and double dating in that car in the mid-'60s.

After spending a wonderful time my first year in college, I was back home in 1966 for a few months before enlisting in the army. Surviving boot camp and numerous other training activities across the country, I ended up at Fort McClellan, Ala., in the spring of 1967. I sensed my father was getting tired of making the trek every other weekend or so to Anniston to bring me home for a visit with family, so eventually he offered to let me buy a new car from his old friend Haynie Gourley, who worked at Capitol Chevrolet on Broadway in Nashville. With extra cash from a college fund that went unused, I selected a 1967 Camaro Super Sport coupe with a 396-cubic-inch, 325-horsepower engine.

Guess my Dad had no idea how fast the car was or anything much about it. I drove it off the showroom floor. It was plum colored, had black interior with bucket seats and a four-on-the-floor gearshift. It was a two-door with a tiny back seat, small trunk but a huge hood. There was a white strip that adorned the concealed, roll-in headlights. The "SS" and checkered flag emblem added the finishing touches. Mashing the pedal to the floor would thrust all to the back of the seats. When using 100-octane gasoline it was, as a close buddy said, a beast.

An original poster for the 1967 movie "Hot Rods To Hell."

After several months I was transferred to Fort Campbell, Ky., and settled into a duty schedule of two days on and three days off, followed by vice-versa the next week. I would make the 60-mile trek home on those days and rendezvous with friends. On one of those early summer days in Nashville, my close friend Dave and I were headed out Franklin Road not too far from town when, as he recalls: "This car that was obviously souped-up pulled next to us. These guys weren't total dumb asses, but they were calling us out. Big mistake. From light to light [Tom] humbled these guys. After about three stoplights the guy in the passenger seat leans out of the window and says 'Man, that's a real road dog!' That car was a wolf in sheep's clothing until you would see the 396 emblem—by then it was too late."

> *Take you for a ride man, it's really a treat,*
> *Strap yourself into a bucket seat.*
> *The four-speed tranny is starting to whine,*
> *You'll know about the Super Sport once we get off the line.*
> *Cruising the highway, getting my kicks,*
> *Nothing can match my...SS 396."*
> —Paul Revere and the Raiders, "SS 396" (1965)

That Camaro was fun to drive but also attracted law enforcement. I was pulled over for suspected bank robbery and subsequently detained somewhere between Ashland City and Fort Campbell in a trooper's back seat with a growling German Shepherd in the front waiting to sample my flesh. I think it was just a ruse to examine my car. The excuse was that the vehicle fit the description of the robber (sure). After a long 30 minutes I was set free.

In another unfortunate incident on a drive back to base, a Clarksville officer stopped me on Highway 12, claiming he had to go over 100 mph to catch me. I disputed that I had broken the speed limit, telling him he could have gone 120 to catch me but that it was irrelevant how fast he had to go. Taking extreme exception to my remarks, he impounded my ride and whisked me into the luxurious Clarksville jail. In a scene that would do justice to a Bela Lugosi film, I was ushered through a large iron door with tiny squares allowing bits of sunlight to filter down a long concrete staircase leading underground, where upon I was confined in a block room with two other sorry souls. They were in for aggravated assault, so when questioned what I was in for I said the same thing plus resisting arrest. I did not want to admit I was in there for a speeding violation, for those men appeared to be seasoned criminals. My First Sergeant Casey rescued me. The final disposition was "not guilty" but I was fined for impudence. They had me either way.

My first date with my wife was in that car, as was as our honeymoon drive to New Orleans in December 1967. While I was off on my Asian "vacation" during 1968, she loved to just hop in it, roll down the windows, turn up the radio and drive. Unfortunately she was broad sided while following my mother on a shopping trip to Cain Sloan in Green Hills. Our 396 was demolished, but she survived. It was a tough time, but we navigated through it. The checkered flag emblem on the side was all that was left.

By the end of the 1960s, the muscle cars and the high-powered "pony cars" (Camaros and Mustangs) started to wane due to the doubling of gasoline prices in the 1970s and '80s. The Chevy 396, 427 and 409s along with the Ford 390, 427 and the Chrysler 440 and 426 Hemi rides all quit production, and the heyday of hot rods and muscle cars starting fading away. Just like the bicycle had liberated us from early childhood, those magnificent American rides freed us of supervision and instilled a feeling of power, independence and perpetual youth never before felt. It was a tough time for parents but a good time for us kids.

> *Well, I wound it up to 110*
> *Twist the speedometer off at the end*
> *I had my foot feed clear to the floor*
> *Said that's all there is*
> *And there ain't no more*
> *Well, they arrested me and put me in jail*
> *I called my pop to go my bail*
> *He said, 'Son, you're gonna drive me to drinking*
> *If you don't quit driving that Hot Rod Lincoln.'"*
> —Charlie Ryan and the Timberline Riders,
>   "Hot Rod Lincoln" (1955)

CHAPTER 10

The Soldier and the Coed

T HE YEAR 1966 marked my first full year as a soldier in the United States Army, having received that designation for my efforts, or lack thereof, from a small, ocean-side, junior college in Bradenton, Fla. As a result, for the next nine months I had the pleasure of residing at Army bases in Kentucky, Missouri, Texas, Alabama and back to Kentucky at Fort Campbell in the spring of 1967. My duty schedule was three days on and two off, and vice versa. I was only 60 miles from Nashville, so on my non-working days I jumped in my plum-colored, 1967 Chevy Camaro SS and blistered it to my home on Cantrell Avenue. I was well aware of the fraternity parties at Vandy, so I usually ended up there. Trying to hold onto my past life, I also visited the homes of old high school acquaintances who were coming back for summer break.

The year 1967 was tumultuous. The "hippie" movement neared its peak, and the "Tune in, Turn on and Drop out" mantra of LSD-advocate Timothy Leary began to resonate with rebellious high-schoolers and college kids. Protests against the Vietnam War raged and soldiers like me were not regarded with high esteem. Black Power advocate Stokely Carmichael spoke in town inciting unrest. "The Summer of Love" ensued as psychedelic music, unbridled sex, drugs, peace and flower children all made the news.

I was especially disappointed that I only skirted the fringes of the free-love movement. Girls asking guys out would have been heaven for me, as my shyness sometimes prevented me from making a call. Besides, a kid in the Army was not considered part of the "In Crowd." The title of the Buckingham's song "Kind of a Drag" fit my life at the time.

July saw sports announcer Larry Munson leave Nashville for Georgia. Cain-Sloan had a big advertising campaign pushing bridal lingerie, and

WSM weatherman Boyce Hawkins had an orchestra that played for a number of social functions. The Association's hits "Windy" and "Cherish" were always on the radio. "The Letter" was a huge song at that time. Procol Harem's "Whiter Shade of Pale" and Jefferson Airplane's "White Rabbit" contrasted with Frank and Nancy Sinatra's "Something Stupid." "Western Union" and "Light My Fire" frequented the airwaves. "Sweet Soul Music" by Arthur Conley, and Sam and Dave's "Soul Man"

The wedding of Carolyn Selph and author Tom Henderson III on Dec. 15, 1967.

were big party tunes. Johnny Rivers was there, and The Electric Prunes sang "I Had Too Much to Dream Last Night." Yes, the country was changing and music personified it.

A life-long friend, Rick Chambers, who went to Hillsboro High and was then at Auburn and home for the summer, thought I would be a good match for a former classmate of his, Carolyn Selph, now in her second year at Peabody College. Telling me I had a blind date put me on edge as I had three of those back in my early teens, none of which resulted in any kind of achievement. Two involved automotive mishaps, one of which resulted in my date becoming awash in pink lemonade and a splattering of strawberry pie. I had waved to some friends in another vehicle while cruising at the Thompson Lane Shoney's and failed to notice that the 1962 Ford in front of me had come to a complete stop. I suspect my folks got the dry cleaning tab.

Rick told me Carolyn was very attractive and a good person on top of that. She had modeled in her early teens at Cain-Sloan and more recently for Castner Knott in the "Flicks of '66 College Board" promotion. She had appeared on stage at the War Memorial "Back-to-School Fashion Show" in August that included the Seventeen Magazine fashion editor, two bands, a singing star, and 70 other models. MaryDe Heckman was one of those and said they were paid $54 for

Carolyn Selph, the author's future wife, in a modeling photo for Caster Knott department store.

their modeling efforts. Even the governor's son, Frank Clement, strutted out on stage. It was a big event. On top of that Carolyn was a former Hillsboro High cheerleader.

All of this led me to wonder why she was available and what would possess her to take a blind date with a guy in the Army. I felt this could be a debacle.

A confirming phone call as to the pick-up time at her home was pleasant enough, leading to some restrained optimism. I had the innate ability to tell within the first few minutes if this was to be a great night or if I should start drinking heavily. Brenton Wood's "Just Gimmie a Little Sign Girl" was all I was looking for that night.

I was a fairly-attractive young man, especially when I had a full head of hair. However, my Troy-Donahue look had disappeared with a buzz cut in Basic Training. That aside, I was witty and fun-loving but pretty much a non-conformist.

My pre-date prep did not include slathering on Brut or Jade East cologne, and I rarely used English Leather. Hai Karate affected my sinuses and not my love life as the ad proclaimed. Occasionally a little Canoe or British Sterling would be applied, but I was more of an Old Spice, Mennen or Ice Blue Aqua Velva kid. My complexion was good, so the odorous Clearasil was not a factor. I avoided joining a fraternity so there were no ascots or pledge pins in my past. My Camaro would help on this date for it had bucket seats. This would eliminate the predicament of how far over towards me she should slide.

I arrived to pick her up at her home on Draughon Avenue on a mid-July night. A knock on the door and a brief wait were followed by an unlatching sound. The front door opened, and she emerged—blue eyes, a sexy smile, and knockout good looks. I was in the presence of a real "fox" that hot summer evening.

The small talk went extremely well, and she even laughed at some of my off-the-wall drivel. We headed over to Richard Cooper's parents' new home on Wilsonia a few miles away, allowing her alluring fragrance of Shalimar perfume to flow through my car. It was unforgettable. Richard was housesitting until his mother could move in. Rick was there along with several others I knew with their dates in tow. No adults and a large home to entertain in made the situation for a blind date ideal. The hi-fi was loaded with records from Hendrix to Mathis, and there was plenty of alcohol to numb any negative vibrations. The large backyard and adjoining patio allowed for privacy, and there were enough of our acquaintances to seek shelter with should this date head south.

Fortunately it went north fast. I'm not sure what happened. It was either the Baccardi Rum or I flipped the right switch. Maybe both. Whatever it was, it was a great night.

By our third date we became what they called in high school "going steady." In college it was called "pinned." We became serious when she broke a date with her current interest to be in my company. He didn't look at me the same afterward, so I made sure to never turn my back on him for a while. The Turtles recording of "She Had Rather Be with Me" would have been appropriate. She and I became inseparable for the next few months and the hit sound "Can't Take My Eyes off You" by Frankie Valli resonated.

Carolyn and Tom arrive at his parents' house after a four-mile walk in the snow from the Oxford House at Vanderbilt on Jan. 15, 1968.

During this period a talking mynah bird was a fixture at Chester's in Green Hills. It used to tell people to "go shop at Cain-Sloan." "American Bandstand" celebrated its tenth anniversary, and you could get in free to a bunch of theatres with six RC bottle caps. November and December sparked hayrides in Warner Park by sororities. The massive 100 Oaks Shopping Center opened, and the James Gang played at Vandy's Delta House. The ZBT fraternity featured a psychedelic float in the homecoming parade. Doug Clark and the Hot Nuts (the paper used the name "Hot Ones" to avoid complaints) played around town, as did Charlie McCoy and the Escorts, The Saturns, Charades, Shifters and The Exotics. The natural look was in for young girls, meaning nothing was worn underneath. It was a good time to be a single male. Life could not have been better for either of us.

All of that ended abruptly upon my receiving a notice stating I would be deploying for one year to CuChi, Vietnam, and to depart the states on the 22nd of January 1968.

I saw the end of Carolyn and me. I was upset and dreaded telling her. When I did she was distraught, but after a brief grief period she concluded we should get married. She knew full well that her mother would have no part of her coming to see me in six months when I would receive my R&R (rest and recuperation) in Hawaii if we were single. In my nonchalant manner I agreed, and that was it. It was the best decision I ever made.

We married on Dec. 15, the same day Bob Hope and Raquel Welch left for Vietnam to entertain the troops. That night we drove for a brief get-a-way

Nero's Cactus Canyon in Green Hills, the scene of Tom and Carolyn's "goodbye" dinner. (Johnny Griswold)

to the Holiday Inn Rivermont in Memphis (interrupted at midnight by two friends playing "In the Midnight Hour" over the phone). That was followed by a drive to New Orleans for New Year's Eve. What a great time we had at the famous Monteleone Hotel (we had no windows in our room). We went to Pat O'Brien's, Clarence "Frog Man" Henry's place and then to Al Hirt's. We ran onto packed Bourbon Street at midnight and hung on to each other amidst the mass of humanity. The Sugar Bowl followed, then we returned home to live in an apartment on the fifth floor of the Oxford House across from the Peabody campus.

It was a great few months and blissful 30 days of marriage. The six-inch snow Jan. 14 enticed us to walk about four miles to my parents' home and further enhanced our brief time together. We were just young kids enjoying our lives in the moment. Sadly, our time together was ending. We decided to dine out for the last time at our favorite spot, Nero's Cactus Canyon. After a lengthy intimate conversation, and a great meal, we held hands and walked out into the cold with heavy hearts. We solemnly moved along the wooden porch to our car. Evidence of the recent snowfall still lingered about. Just as we got to the end of the walkway, saddened by our imminent separation the next day, a patch of ice caused our feet to go out from under us simultaneously. We both immediately fell onto our hindquarters with both legs hanging off the small ledge at the end of the walkway. It looked as though we had just taken a seat. Our hands remained clasped. We looked at each other and, sensing no injury, hugged and broke out in laughter and then tears. I knew right then we would make it.

The next day arrived too soon, and the time had finally come to say goodbye. I was not sure a one-year separation would work or if I would even survive.

As I prepared to leave the terminal at Berry Field on Jan. 20, 1968, we embraced so long that it made the boarding manager uncomfortable. He finally cleared his throat, and we slowly separated. I gave him my ticket, moved through the turnstile, crossed the tarmac and boarded the airliner. It was the worst moment of my life. The lyrics of a song recorded that year by Peter, Paul and Mary said it all:

> *So kiss me and smile for me*
> *Tell me that you'll wait for me*
> *Hold me like you'll never let me go*
> *'Cause I'm leavin' on a jet plane*
> *Don't know when I'll be back again*
> *Oh babe, I hate to go*

Tears welled up as I took my seat and the aircraft started moving down the runway. I remembered the past few months, the parties, the closeness, the smell of Shalimar, the wedding-night phone call, the New Year's Eve on Bourbon Street, and the slip and fall at Nero's. The times were changing, but in my case not for the worse. For you see, my life was forever transformed, enriched, and made whole by a beautiful, blue-eyed college coed with a sexy smile who became my wife.

CHAPTER 11

Skate, Wrestle
and Rock

L EAVING A beautiful wife after being married less than 45 days, for a
year-long stay in Southeast Asia in 1968, was a low point in my life. Not
only was the country in a state of flux, but my way of life for 21 years was
rudely interrupted. On top of that, pieces of my childhood were beginning
to fade away.

In January 1968, the Nashville Banner's Red O'Donnell wrote: "Shed a
roller-bearing tear, mates—the Hippodrome Skating Rink is about to slide
into oblivion." By March 1968 the old-timers were gathering for what they
called their "Final Skate Party."

*The Hippodrome rink as it appeared in 1958. To the left of the front doors is a concession stand
advertising popcorn and hot dogs. Seating used for other activities, such as wrestling matches and
musical performances, can be seen on the left and right. (Nashville Public Library, Nashville Room, photo
by Jack Gunter)*

Built in 1905, the Hippodrome Roller Rink was located at 2613 West End Avenue across from Centennial Park. It is pictured here in February 1968 not long before being demolished. The sign to the left of the entrance reads: "Skating, Every Night 7:45 to 10:00." (Nashville Public Library, Nashville Room, photo by Charles W. Warterfield)

The Hippodrome Roller Rink, at 2613 West End Ave. across from Centennial Park, was built in 1905 by W.P. Ready and sold to Tony Sudekum, the famous movie-house baron. At 100 feet wide by 350 feet long, the facility was enormous, with seating up to 20,000 and 40 exits should a mass evacuation be needed. Covering 4 1/2 acres, it was the largest auditorium in the region and was even nicknamed "The Madison Square Garden of the South."

It featured mirrored walls and a 40-foot ornamental plaster ceiling sporting thousands of lights. At times you could see your face in the polished maple floor. There was a dance hall in the back and a balcony in the front containing a kindergarten and beginner's skating rink. Solid-wood railings ran lengthwise separating the seating from the main floor (and supporting those just learning to skate). There was a soda fountain on a raised platform and a full-service skate locker.

On the outside, numerous steps ascended to a grand entrance with a canopy displaying the words "Roller Rink" in the middle and "Hippodrome" on either side. The building itself had huge letters spelling out "Hippodrome" across the front. (In later years the Hippodrome Barber Shop was next door where my neighborhood friend's father, David Slabosky, was a regular customer.)

Through the years the Hippodrome served many purposes. It was home to a Depression-era Walk-A-Thon, and for a quarter one could skate all day. You could watch Vanderbilt basketball. You could see big bands such as Duke Ellington, Harry James, Guy Lombardo, The Dorseys, Glenn Miller, Artie Shaw and the like, many of whom were brought in by soon-to-be-wrestling-promoter Nick Gulas. There were Golden-Gloves boxing matches, high school dances, Clinic Bowl coronations, Nashville's first indoor baseball game, and in 1955 it was the site of the largest dinner ever held by the Democratic Party. It had its own Nativity Scene in 1949 and hosted the Christmas Village in 1964. If you had a loved one nearing the Promised Land, you could even view the latest in caskets at the State Funeral Directors Show. It was Nashville's top entertainment venue.

I missed out on the Walk-A-Thon, was not around to see the Big Band

Fats Domino plays at the Hippodrome in May 1959. (Nashville Public Library, Nashville Room, photo by Jack Gunter)

acts and sadly did not attend the Funeral Director's show. But what I did witness at that old facility is still fresh in the memory bank.

Although not yet 6 years old, I went with some other kids back in the early 1950s to see wrestling up close and personal. This particular match drew a packed house of intoxicated fanatics. The combatants, I believe, were Lou Thesz and Gorgeous George. The entire ring was enclosed in crude chicken wire, the kind with the large holes in it. At the peak of the match a one-armed, wheelchair-bound, inebriated lady stood up and chucked what looked to be a brick over the wire and onto the mat. Amidst the smoke-filled auditorium, security personnel appeared and escorted both her and the wheelchair out of the area. This caused an eruption of boos, slurs and unidentifiable objects to be thrown at those folks. A fight broke out midway down the aisle and the attention of the crowd moved to the commotion. Our parental chaperone felt we had seen enough, so an abrupt departure was made out one of the 40 exits. I don't think I ever went back to see wrestling again.

Original headline and caption from the May 5, 1959, Nashville Banner: "Cool, Man, Cool!— Sheer ecstasy, with a tinge of enthusiasm, is etched on the face of this rock and roll fan at the Hippodrome, where singer Antoine (Fats) Domino and his band provided a steady beat for scores of dancing couples, who happily roared through the evening to the background of Domino's recording hits." (Nashville Public Library, Nashville Room, photo by Jack Gunter)

An interior shot of the Hippodrome during the May 1959 Fats Domino performance. (Nashville Public Library, Nashville Room, photo by Jack Gunter)

That was probably a good thing, for not long after that The Green Shadow was smacked in the noggin with a bottle of Coke after he attacked his tag-team partner, who was a crowd favorite. The Shadow was whisked out of the ring followed by a frenzied throng, said to be in the thousands, where they proceeded to tear down the walls of his dressing room, prompting the Nashville Riot Squad to be called in. Teargas facilitated his escape but caused a near stampede of tanked-up fans.

Tuesday-night wrestling promoted by Nick Gulas vacated the Hippodrome in 1952 and relocated to the State Fairgrounds where similar shenanigans continued. Other wrestling matches continued at the Hippodrome for years to come.

Throughout the 1950s and '60s music was a big draw. In 1959, Fats Domino with his many hit songs, Clyde McPhatter ("A Lover's Question"), The Crests ("16 Candles"), and Chubby Checker ("The Twist") all performed there. Those shows were advertised as being for whites only.

That same year I had just become interested in records but was too young to see Bo Diddley in action. Again that was probably a good thing, I guess, for mayhem erupted when a teenager from Antioch broke into some lewd and suggestive dance moves during one of Bo's hard-driving sounds (see photo on facing page). Young males naturally became excited and joined in. This was not the fox trot or the Tennessee Waltz we had mastered at Tweensters or Fortnightly dance studios. It was a wild body shake—like an amped-up combination of the Hand Jive and the Madison, both pre-cursors of the Monkey. One news account stated: "While being arrested she slapped Officer York across his head causing his hat to sail twenty feet over the crowd."

Original headline and caption from the Nov. 13, 1959, Nashville Banner: "Jaihouse Rock: Bonnie Ann Roberts— Her Dancing 'a Common Exhibition?'" (Nashville Public Library, Nashville Room, photo by Vic Cooley)

Big acts continued to perform into the 1960s. James Brown, The Drifters, Marvin Gaye, Major Lance, Ruby & The Romantics, and Jimmy Reed were all part of the 16-act show in 1963. Sam Cooke and Jackie Wilson performed in 1964. Later, "Louie Louie" was performed by The Kingsmen, and Sam the Sham & The Pharaohs did their "Wooly Bully" and "Little Red Riding Hood" numbers. In-state artists The Gentrys ("Keep on Dancing") also made an appearance. The Hippodrome was truly a major music hall back then.

Dancing, concerts, wrestling, conventions, Walk-A-Thons and rock 'n' roll shows graced the Hippodrome, but this magnificent structure was known as the best roller-skating rink in the south. Parents took their kids with them on the weekends. Carolyn (Selph) Henderson remembers going with her parents and sister in the mid-'50s. Her mom could skate but her dad could do a backward glide at the same speed—an impressive sight for a young kid.

Our elementary school and many others across the city had class skating parties, usually centered around a child's birthday and supervised by watchful parents.

Climbing those steps to the entrance was exciting. Soon you would hear the organ music and see the lights. Gradually the smell of popcorn and perspiring skaters all blended together with warm shoe leather. I knew that eventually I would feel the rush of air blowing my unbuttoned shirt and the wheels beneath my feet whizzing over the golden wood floor. I would hurry in, go to the skate check-out counter, and get my clamp-ons. There was a skate attendant—an older man with some kind of affliction—who regularly adjusted the skates over my penny loafers. Girls always had those pink or white high-boot skates, which I thought made their legs look long and pretty.

I became a fairly proficient skater due to numerous parties and practicing some on our concrete basketball court at home.

From the June 12, 1962, Nashville Banner: "Sandra Stiles (Miss Hippodrome) rehearses a 'lift' with her skating partner James Duke while the 1961 Southern Regional Junior Skating-Dance Champions Margo Vaughan and Bobby Travis work on their routine. The Southern Regional Roller Skating Championships will be held from June 17 through June 21 at the Hippodrome with skaters from seven states competing." (Nashville Public Library, Nashville Room, photo by Jack Gunter)

Ben West Jr. (far right), the son of the mayor, celebrates his birthday at the Hippodrome in March 1952. (Nashville Metro Archives)

During one birthday party, while in the fourth grade at Woodmont School, I finally got the hang of it and forever moved away from pulling myself meekly along the rail. As soon as the "All Skate" announcement was given, informing every roller that any and everyone could enter center stage, friend Ralph and I immediately left our cake, donut, Coke and popcorn-covered table and hit the rink. The organ music picked up a notch as we breezed at breakneck speeds past slower kids and groups of girls holding hands for support. There were a few instances when we would come too close to those groups and make brief but disastrous contact. This often resulted in a gasping, spasmodic fall by one, starting a domino collapse of all and ending in a pile of dresses, ponytails and boot skates. No injuries occurred, but the Hippodrome's "Skate Boy" monitor took note and chased us down. Punishment was like being given a penalty for high-sticking. Our placement outside the rails in a virtual penalty box until we could straighten up proved futile, I'm afraid.

Those who went later in the day or at night—teenagers, young adults, engaged couples, those wanting to be engaged couples, families, old-timers and the like—were treated to a less noisy and more restrained crowd. Experience reigned and many times the floor was vacated for the sharply-dressed regulars who had choreographed routines to soothing organ music. It was ice-skating on wheels. Twirling, splits, and hand-holding moves prevailed. I was not a part of that group.

The Grand March was quite a show, and often the 1954 romantic hit "Goodnight Sweeheart," recorded by the Spaniels, would be played at the end of the night.

Local and regional skating championships were highly publicized and there was even an annual crowning of a Miss Hippodrome, a young girl whose roller skills and beauty were the envy of all.

As land values increased and the times began to change, this magnificent facility slowly became a liability. After 60-plus years of skating, wrestling, music, sporting events and shows of all kinds, the Hippodrome left us. To those who were the Hippodrome—Joe Oehmig, Porter Woolwine, Mary Jo Bartgatze, Evelyn Vaughn, Gertrude Gregory, Moe, Ham, Connie, and the afflicted man who attached my skates, the "Skate Boys" and monitors who put me in the penalty box, W.P. Ready, Tony Sudekum and anyone that ever worked there—I say with a smile and a reflective sadness what soul legends Sam and Dave sang in March of 1968, "I Thank You."

CHAPTER 12

December 1970

SITTING IN the third row at a Jimi Hendrix concert in 1969, my wife and I had a kid next to us say, to no one in particular, "I'm tripping out." It saddened me, not for the youth necessarily but for what was happening to the times. Hendrix overdosed in 1970, as did Janis Joplin. Boxing great Sonny Liston also died that year. Four Kent State students were fatally shot during an anti-war protest.

On the radio Smokey Robinson belted out "Tears of a Clown" and the Vietnam protest song "War" by Edwin Starr became a hit. The Carpenters were the next great singing duo sharing the limelight with Simon and Garfunkel. There were groups called Sugarloaf, Ides of March, Three Dog Night and Black Oak Arkansas on the scene. We saw Black Oak in Memphis on several occasions, once with Three Dog Night as smoldering cannabis was passed down the aisle. It was high times at the Liberty Bowl.

In theaters the movies ranged from "M*A*S*H," "Airport" and "Patton" to "Gimme Shelter" (documenting the tragic Altamont Rock Festival featuring the Rolling Stones).

There was racial unrest, increasing drug use, and Charles Manson with his deranged Helter Skelter followers were put on trial for the Hollywood murders of Sharon Tate and the LaBiancas.

The good old '50s and '60s of our misspent youth had faded away.

It was the '70s.

Although I was married in 1967, 1970 was our first full year of being a couple away from Nashville (other than a three-month stint in Denver) because of my military commitment and her final semester at Peabody. We had moved to Memphis in the fall of '69 where I enrolled at Memphis State and

The author and his wife, Carolyn, stand in front of their Memphis apartment (notice the number) with two of their dogs, Bogey and Princess, in December 1970.

my wife became employed by the Memphis school system as a special-education teacher instructing homebound kids who were ill and unable to attend class. She drove our blue 1968 Volkswagen hatchback with its trunk uniquely located in the front of the vehicle, which was great for carrying extra stuff and freeing up space in the car for our dog Bogey, who rode with her to appointments on occasion. We even put a peace symbol on our gas tank cover just to placate the university crowd.

We took up residence in the Yorktown courtyard apartment complex at 3780 Cape Henry Drive in the outlying area of Raleigh. Our apartment, No. 13, was available probably because of the Triskaidekaphobia syndrome (fear of the number 13). The number 13 was not significant to me at the time.

We were situated adjacent to tennis courts, a large field with overgrown backwoods, marshes and a creek that was inaccessible. You could legally fire a shotgun back there if desired, which I did on occasion. It was only a stone's throw from our door and was ideal for slinging the Frisbee for Bogey, which was his passion. Our passions were each other, partying with new friends and enjoying life. To paraphrase the Carpenters, "We had only just begun."

I guess it was our upbringing and love of animals that often caused some tense times. I cannot speak for my wife, but I believe that it was my paternal

grandmother with
her chickens, stray
cats and numerous
dogs that ingrained
in me a compassion
for these creatures.

St. Francis of
Assisi, the patron
saint of animals,
must have alerted
the local animal
kingdom that we
had temporarily
moved to Memphis,
for soon after arriv-

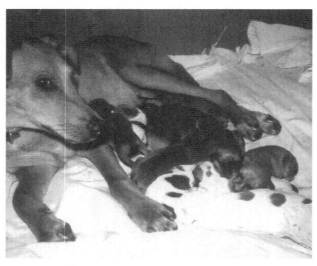

Princess eyes the camera as she feeds some of her 13 puppies, newly born on Christmas Eve 1970.

ing a mixed hound with a crushed hip wandered up from the marshes. After a day or two I could not stand to see the dog go hungry, so I brought it in, gave it a bath in Prell shampoo, fed it and put a towel down for it to rest. Our dog Bogey must have had some of Assisi's blood in his makeup because he accepted it without incident, just as he did with others that were to come. Terry, as we called him, never really recovered, although he did benefit from proper nourishment. Eventually he had to be put down. Soon after that a fox terrier we named Tippy, due to the white tip on his tail, came calling. After a week or two of our free hospitality, another resident adopted him after seeing the notice we placed on the bulletin board in the communal laundry area. Chalk up a good ending to that one.

As if orphaned dogs were not enough, the avian community must have heard about our benevolences and flew in. On my way to class one morning I noticed a robin sitting on the yellow line between two lanes of traffic. It failed to move as I whizzed past, and it bobbled in the wind. Thinking it had been gravely injured I "u-turned" and went back to make sure there was no more misery it had to endure. Upon further review it appeared to be only stunned. Stopping traffic I picked up the red bird, held it in my left hand, partially steered with my knees, shifted gears with my right, and drove to the nearest

Tom and Carolyn enjoy the puppies while they can. An announcement on 650AM ensured that all 13 Christmas-Eve pups found homes.

vet. When I entered, the receptionist was a bit taken back and told me to take a seat.

Moments later my patient regained its senses, escaped my clutches, and circled the room at breakneck speeds. There were shrieks from an elderly, fine-ly-dressed matron as my robin red-breast dropped a deposit very close to, and perhaps in, her bluish hair. I rushed to the door, threw it open and out the bird flew, much to everyone's delight. I turned and said, "You can cancel the exam."

Life returned to normalcy until around my 24th birthday on Dec. 3. Not long after enjoying the luscious cake Carolyn made and celebrating another year of existence, we discovered an extremely malnourished, nursing (or so we thought), mixed-breed dog in the field behind our complex. We had no choice but to bring in this near-death pooch. After a week or two of baths, fine vittles and proper care we discovered that she, whom we named Princess, was not nursing but was in a motherly way.

Christmas vacation was upon us, and we were coming back home to Nashville for the holidays. There was no choice but to load everyone, Princess included, into our VW and head to Davidson County. The two dogs rode in our back seat. Only one morning sickness incident occurred during the commute somewhere between Jackson and Cuba Landing in the middle of I-40. No need for a detailed explanation. We spent the holidays at my boyhood home on Cantrell Avenue, and thanks to

The Hendersons' 1968 Volkswagen hatchback is shown here with its front trunk lid open and packed for a trip.

wonderful parents all were accepted. Bogey and Kris, my once Christmas cocker spaniel and now my parents' tenant, had the entire house to roam while Princess was placed in our basement next to the coal-burning furnace, with more than sufficient accoutrements around her, I might add.

Nashville was in its usual festive, goodwill mood as street decorations and shoppers flocked to all the downtown department stores. The popular board game Yahtzee was selling for just $1.88 at Harvey's and all pets were on sale for 40 percent off at Docktor Pet Center in 100 Oaks. "Love Story" was to open at the Martin Theater on Christmas Day. The soul girl group The Shirelles had just performed at the Safari Club on Hayes Street and a new singing group called the Jackson 5 was to give a holiday performance at the Municipal Auditorium. The Tennessean caption read "...and the lead singer is only 9 years old." The Fannie Battle Carolers were readying for their neighborhood mission with their slogan "A candle in every window, a carol at every door." The temperature had dropped from a record high of 72 on the 23rd to a frigid 23 degrees on Christmas Eve just in time to give everyone that holiday feel.

The Nashville Banner reported that there had been an increase of 2 percent in the state birth rate for the year. The "Cradle Roll" column listed approximately 50 new births on Christmas Eve but did not take into account what was beginning to transpire in the basement at 700 Cantrell Ave.

My mother descended the steps from the breakfast room in mid-morning to do some laundry, then yelled back up the stairs: "Princess is having her baby!" What an understatement. Our abandoned orphan kept them coming, and by nightfall 13 pups had arrived. It was more than a three-dog night. There were brown, black, brown and white, black and white, fuzzy and some with very little hair. Princess evidently got around. All survived thanks to some help from Mom and others who came by. I am certainly glad no one suffered from that dreaded Triskaidekaphobia.

Christmas Day was overwhelming but busy and was the event of the year for our family and friends.

Ironically, two films debuted that day in Nashville with a cat-themed title. Walt Disney's "The Aristocats" opened at the Melrose Theater ("It's a feline frolic") and "The Owl and the Pussycat" showcasing Barbara Streisand and George Segal began a run at the Belcourt Theater. Neither felines nor owls would have fared well in our basement. Princess was quite protective.

A couple of weeks passed as my mother regularly made trips to H.G. Hills for liver to cook so that Princess would have the required iron to feed all of her offspring. She and Carolyn even hand-fed via baby bottle the ones that were puny. Quite a saintly undertaking, I must say.

It was fortunate that my father worked for National Life and Accident Insurance Company, parent company of WSM, for those good souls at 650 on the a.m. radio dial broadcast news of the multiple births over the 50,000 watt powerhouse, proclaiming that the Hendersons had 13 free puppies born on Christmas Eve available for pick up on a first-come, first-serve basis. After four weeks every pup was given a good home to strangers who ventured down our basement steps. Princess was adopted by my sister Lynn and her husband.

The 1970 Christmas "break" finally came to a close. By the middle of January 1971 Mom, Dad, and their dog Kris regained some sanity, and life returned to normal.

A good feeling swept over us as we returned back down I-40 to resume life on the outskirts of Memphis in apartment No. 13. When time eventually runs out and Carolyn and I take our last breath, I trust we will be looked upon favorably by the powers that be, just as I am sure my parents were. Should there be any questions or objections, a robin, numerous abandoned dogs, Princess, St. Francis and 13 puppies will be more than happy to give glowing recommendations.

CHAPTER 13

A Neighborhood
School

WOODMONT SCHOOL began classes on Sept. 30, 1931, "with a competent corps of teachers" (so said the Nashville Banner). The first-through-eighth-grade facility was well lighted, properly ventilated (no air-conditioning in those days) and above all had steam heat. It also had a modern cafeteria in the basement complete with kitchen and serving areas. Concerned citizens of this 7th District in southwest Davidson County raised $3,000 to earn the backing of school board member Dan Mills. Lurton Goodpasture headed up the successful drive that occurred, amazingly enough, during the Great Depression. In 1934 the Banner displayed a picture stating, "Children who attend Woodmont School…find the work inside as pleasant as the exterior of the building is attractive." Mrs. G.C. Mathis was selected as the first principal of this neighborhood school that would become part of my family's life from 1934 until I left in 1959.

In 1953 the first day of school was Sept. 1, a hot day that reached a record-setting 102 degrees. There was still no air-conditioning, but students and teachers alike made it through. I walked to school that day carrying a satchel containing some school supplies and my lunch (I later got a metal, cowboy-hero lunch box). The school was only three blocks from my house, so I and a couple of friends, who all lived on the same street, walked together with our parents trailing behind. Woodmont's reputation had attracted scores of homeowners into the area bringing with them hundreds of young children.

Coming down the big hill on Wilson Avenue you would turn into the backside of the property, go across the playground, and down a few concrete steps to a long paved area that slowly descended to the first grade classrooms on the left side of the building. To the right was an entrance to the main part

Woodmont School in 1934. (Nashville Metro Archives)

of the school which took you past the infirmary. On the first day it invariably contained some poor child lying on a cot with a wash cloth on his head.

On entering my first-grade classroom for the first time I was introduced to my teacher, Ella Lee Thomas. She frightened me, as she appeared to be very stern and orderly, a far cry from my disposition. I quickly learned that there would be no foolishness in her class as Bruce Gold and I were made to put our noses in a carefully drawn circle on the blackboard and leave them there without moving until we had learned our lesson. It was worse for others. John Tompkins was so disturbed about school that he ran away crying.

There were 33 kids in my class, and 32 in the other first-grade class, taught by Mrs. Elsie Hows.

Somehow I managed to get through the first day and eventually became accustomed to the schedule. There was always a devotional, a pledge, then language and social studies, followed by health, lunch and recess. At the end of recess our teacher always made us lay our heads down on our desks and be quiet for 30 minutes. Despite the occasional giggle and whisper it was no trouble to rest as the heat and effects of lunch and exercise caused a warm feeling and heavy eyelids to overtake us all. I am sure this gave our teacher a much-needed break as well.

Skills were the next exercise, which was mainly learning to write within the lines of our oversized tablet. The lines appeared to be several inches tall and always had a dashed line between the solid ones. The huge No. 1 pencils were so thick my entire palm was filled to capacity.

Our first-grade schedule concluded with games, followed by another rest and an "appreciation period" about how to act

The author (left) and friend, Rhea Sumpter, are pictured on their return from first-grade registration at Woodmont School on Aug. 31, 1953.

toward your elders and fellow classmates. Finally, the teacher did a performance evaluation for the day, culminating in dismissal at 2:30. We would go to the cloak room to gather our empty lunch pails and belongings and prepare to walk home or go to a waiting automobile.

For me there remained only one more thing to do, and that was to stand in line at the school crossing and wait for the official-looking Patrol Boys to lift up their long, bamboo poles upon which hung yellow flags with a bright red STOP written all the way across. Those kids had badges of some kind, making them authority figures to me. Some took advantage of their status by telling us not to run across the road. I was usually in a hurry to see "The Howdy Doody Show," which came on at 3:30 on Channel 4.

Other than lunch, recess was the high point of the day for me. Games of kick ball on the blacktop or a spirited game of dodge ball got most of the aggression out of us. Of course the slow-footed, non-athletic kids were pummeled with those big, bouncy, red rubber balls, usually upside the head. A well-chucked ball at the cranium often brought "ooohhs" from the unscathed. When Red Rover was played, the largest kids plowed through the hand-held line with ease.

At the far end of our playground were primitive-looking seesaws, nothing more than a board balanced on a pipe. The key to a satisfying ride was to be the first one off. But if one bailed too soon your classmate on the other end would plummet to the ground in a bone-jarring fall. No fun at all.

Another few yards away was a large jungle gym, sometimes called monkey bars. This was a one-story contraption featuring several layers of steel bars where kids could climb and hang or sit at different heights while others attempted to do the same. Child safety was, for the most part, disregarded. It was up to the kid to exercise caution. Falling off meant landing in a thin covering of sawdust. Repeatedly throwing sawdust into the air could result in a spanking by the P.E. teacher. I fell into the "repeatedly" bracket often enough that our P.E. instructor, Mr. Alsup, carried a long, wooden paddle emblazoned with my name. It was utilized more than I would have liked.

Girls played hopscotch on the marked blacktop, gathered in groups, watched the more physical action of the boys, or just sat along a nearby creek and talked. That creek was the site of a near tragedy during that time when Buford Frogge attempted to raft the storm-swollen waters and became stuck under a culvert. Emergency personnel were dispatched, attracting onlookers adults and children alike. Fortunately, after much ado, Buford was extracted

Our janitor, Cecil Gentry, was by all accounts the backbone of the school during my tenure and a good guy to all (see following chapter). He was so trusted that he often moonlighted for a number of after-hours social functions involving school parents. He assisted at my home for my oldest sister's wedding reception. Everyone knew and loved Cecil just as they did "Plez," the janitor in the early 1940s. The two were kind in nature, never disciplining, always pleasant and loved us kids.

Looking back on my school, certain things have stuck with me.

The family atmosphere was personified by the large number of parents involved with all aspects of learning. The PTA Executive Board had eight members and 25 committee chairmen. The Men's Club had three officers and six committee chairmen. All eight grades had two room mothers assigned to each teacher. Woodmont School even had a "Joint Committee on Objectionable Comic Books and Obscene Literature," consisting of four members. Mad and Cracked magazines were on the list as were High Society and some of the police gazette periodicals, which made them quite popular.

There were teachers I will never forget. Thomas, Hows, Sherrod, Santi, Doyle, Dixon, Johnson, Brandt, Kain, Bowen, Pollard, Seay, Sams and Warren come to mind. Mrs. Clark was remembered because all the kids in my class thought she was good-looking. My principal from the third grade on was Leonard Garriot, a kind man who was unjustly feared because he had only one arm. I think it was the Captain Hook syndrome. He took the school to county-wide notoriety for as long as I was there.

The classrooms, and later the portables, seemed large with a number of windows opening to a view of the field out back. An expansive blackboard seemed to cover an entire wall. (Why they called it "black" I have no clue, for in fact it was green.) Over the blackboard were pull-down charts, graphs and maps of all kinds. At the bottom of the board was a long tray filled with chalk, dust and erasers. If your deportment was poor, the teacher made you beat the erasers with a yardstick outside after class or just bang them together, to get the dust out. I still have that powdery taste in my mouth. I remember when Jimmy in Mrs. Warren's fourth-grade class threw all of his coins up in the air during rest time. Jimmy wasn't "quite right" and had regular eraser duty.

There were pictures of presidents, a copy of the Declaration of Independence and other patriotic symbols, including an American flag, adorning the room.

In the colder months our steam heat would kick in, provided by glowing, creaking radiators. There were no safety measures to keep children from getting burned. We all knew what would happen if we touched a radiator. However, those steamy heat sources enabled us to melt pencil erasers and other pliable objects. Chewing gum, which was a no-no, melted quickly and filled the air with the pleasant scent of spearmint or Juicy Fruit. But if a piece of Black Jack gum was rendered down, the teacher demanded that the culprit be revealed.

Admittedly there were aspects of life at Woodmont School that I didn't enjoy.

I avoided the Weekly Reader, if possible, because there were too many lessons in there for me to do. I disliked the arts-and-crafts part of class, which seemed to intensify during any seasonal event. I was not much of a cut-and-paster. For every occasion, cut-outs, poster boards and ribbons were constructed to form large exhibits to grace the walls. The white, creamy Elmer's glue was favored by some kids for eating despite repeated teacher warnings. We evidently were not completely trusted as our cutting utensil was a pair of small scissors with extremely blunt ends. No stabbings occurred.

I also avoided the upstairs bathroom as eighth-grade boys made that their hangout and smoking area. A couple of them, Ronnie and Johnny, had motorbikes, which led us younger students to label them as "hoods."

I do, however, regret not spending more time in our library downstairs. I occasionally entered and looked at all the colorful books. "Uncle Remus" was there. The Highlights for Children magazine, featuring Goofus and Gallant, was on a shelf along with an array of Little Golden Books and assorted hard covers. The most intriguing item was a large hornet's nest that was placed in plain view from the hall by our librarian, Mrs. Kershaw. I suspect it was purposely positioned there to attract kids like me.

The cafeteria was the site for a number of events. Just outside the door was a water fountain, which I never used because word was that Charles had put his mouth on the spigot and everyone knew who Charles was. Lunchtime was always special, for after it followed recess. To get there our teachers would lead us from our classroom in an orderly fashion through a small door, arriving at a mountainous stack of off-white, black-and-brown Formica trays. Mrs. McClure, with hair in a bonnet, and several assistants would serve up the day's selections along with those little waxy cartons of milk that pulled apart at the top. The nutritional value of salmon croquettes must have been off the charts, for it appeared three times a week as the main selection. Most of us usually brought a sandwich in our lunch boxes, purchasing the accessories as needed, but always buying those round containers of Velvet ice cream with the tiny protruding tab you had to pull to remove the cover. Let's not forget the little wooden spoons that came with each cup.

Sliding our plastic trays along the long silver shelves while making our daily choice of items and then entering the lunch hall became a social event.

Who and how many friends sat around you quickly determined your popularity, much like the total number of those red-and-white, two-inch-by-four-inch Valentine cards you would get. (Although most of mine came from boys I did get some from Tam, Betty Sue, Susan, Lucy, Butterball and Cathy—see Chapter 15.) Our seats were long benches that only minutes before were concealed in the wall along with the tables. Occasionally someone would upchuck. A chorus of "ooooohs" would erupt, and the guilty party would forever be remembered as having thrown up in the lunch room.

Paul remembers Bob Creighton finding a worm in his milk. That news spread like wildfire throughout the school. And Edward Mendalsohn brought his money in an old sock everyday and endured much ridicule for doing so.

We also watched informative films in the cafeteria. One was on rabies, with graphic depictions of chained monkeys frothing at the mouth; another was about safety precautions to take in the event of an atom bomb hitting nearby; and one tried to convince us of how pleasant it was to take the polio vaccine. Features depicting youngsters displaying proper hygiene, such as how to use a comb and wash your hands, were popular.

Proud parents endured excruciatingly off pitch flute concerts by their youngsters standing on rows of metal bleachers on the cafeteria stage. I could play three notes of "This Old Man," and generally mimed the rest. One time Linda failed to keep her knees unlocked, as we were instructed to do. The reduction of oxygen to her brain resulted in a collapse and tumble to the stage floor, causing quite a stir.

Paul Clements once impersonated the planet Uranus in a class skit on astronomy. Unfortunately the teacher butchered the pronunciation, as Paul remembers, placing the emphasis on the second syllable. Fortunately the young age and knowledge of the other "planets" saved him from future chiding.

The annual auction took place in the cafeteria and packed the room, as did the heralded spaghetti supper. We sold tickets for this event with awards given for the most sales. Elizabeth once got to be principal for a day for her efforts. The annual Christmas play was a high point as students showed their talent, or lack thereof, to an adoring audience. Athletic awards were passed out on the cafeteria stage before the entire school on numerous occasions.

The Woodmont School fourth-grade class of Mrs. Warren in 1956. The author is in the fourth row, first kid from the left.

The Woodmont School Carnival was legendary. Cars lined up for blocks along Compton (later changed to Estes Road), Kenner and Wilson Avenues. The PTA, the Men's Club and involved parents, neighborhood friends and students put on the carnival, which was once described as the best in the county. It always started at dusk, and one could hear the loud speakers blocks away blaring hits of the day, such as Sinatra, Bill Haley and his Comets, Duane Eddy and Ricky Nelson. It was cool, man.

The adults would gather in the cafeteria for bingo and the huge auction. Hazel Tudor said she once bought some sterling earrings for 10 cents.

Crowds line up to enter the "midway" of the 1955 Woodmont School carnival. The school building is on the right, in front of which is a Velvet Ice Cream booth. (Katherine Clements)

There were cake walks, ring toss, rifle shoot, a dunking machine and helium balloons, and the surrounding streets were filled with the smoky aroma of parents charcoaling their specialties. A neighbor, Russell Brothers, whose kids attended Woodmont, had a popular booth selling his locally-owned Velvet Ice Cream to the carnival goers.

A silver Strong Man Machine trimmed in red and yellow with W.G. Bush and Co. on the side was made and furnished by another nearby school supporter and parent, Johnny Herbert of Herbert Materials. This "test your strength" enticement had a very tight, spring-operated lever that when struck by a sledgehammer with sufficient muscle would propel a weight up a tall tower and clang a bell at the top. Unfortunately, no youngster had the go-power to get it done (nor did most adults for that matter), but when someone did succeed all heads turned in amazement. Many boasting high school-ers, often with a girlfriend wearing their letter sweaters, repeatedly failed and were quickly humbled and then promptly ridiculed by youngsters watching in the crowd. I was one of those youngsters. All of these attractions went into making this the event of the year, every year.

Field Day was usually held behind the school on an expansive lot, but on occasion it was held at Herbert's or Brother's Fields three blocks away. The students were divided up into blues and golds. Blue ribbons were given for the fastest runners, the highest jumpers and to those who threw the farthest softball, etc. I never won a blue ribbon in racing because John was always the fastest in our class. His nickname was Mighty Mouse. Not everyone was a winner so our teachers were always there to console those who came up empty-handed. Participation awards did not exist then, so many of us fell into that category.

The years went by quickly. The Boy Scout troop continued to raise and lower Old Glory in the front of the school, and the Patrol Boys exercised their road safety skills twice a day. We graduated from the fat pencils to the thin ones and kept the walls decorated throughout the seasons.

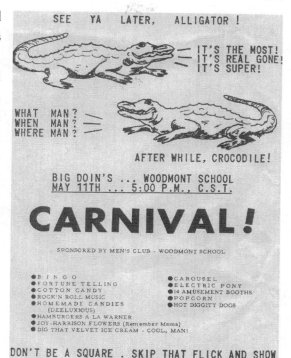

A flyer advertising the 1957 Woodmont School carnival, featuring green ink printed on yellow paper.

Paul Clements (left) and Norman Carl at the 1955 Woodmont School carnival. (Katherine Clements)

First-grade teacher Miss "Elsie" Hows consoles student Phillip Morgan, who, it appears, did not win a competition at the 1952 Woodmont School Field Day. In the background is the author's home at 700 Cantrell Ave. The family car is seen parked in the garage. (Phil Morgan)

Our parents monitored our progress by participating in committees, volunteering as room mothers, organizing the spaghetti supper, carnival, Field Day and spearheading numerous coat-hanger and paper drives. They allowed us the freedom to ride our bikes or walk to school by ourselves, sometimes followed by our faithful dogs. They assisted in school plays, transported us to skating parties at the Hippodrome, and cheered for us at sporting events held at the Onion Bowl and other schools.

The janitors kept our school clean with the familiar-smelling cleaning compound that was applied and buffed on the wooden and linoleum floors. Our teachers came and went but most stayed in their respective classrooms instructing the young minds who followed in our footsteps on how to do division and multiplication, how to read, how to write with those big pencils, and later how to diagram a simple sentence. Above all they instilled in us values that would last a lifetime. The friends made, the characters we met and the experiences we had were all part of this wonderful neighborhood school. Woodmont was like a huge family, an extension of the "Ozzie and Harriet" and "Trouble with Father" television shows.

Busing in 1971 reduced my former school to just four grades, and within

10 years, on May 19, 1981, Principal Francis Kristofferson sent a letter home to all parents stating that the school was closing for good. The bulldozing took place in 1986, and the lot became Woodmont Park in the spring of 1987.

Where I and thousands of children had come to learn and grow up became only a memory. I wish I could recall my last day of school, but like most kids my age I just moved on, looking to the future without thinking about the past.

If given the opportunity to go back to the last time the bell rang for dismissal, I would clean out the supplies from my desk and then shuffle to the cloakroom at the back of the class. There I would pick up my Hopalong Cassidy lunch box, my hooded, bright-yellow raincoat with the black clasps, and any excess clothing left behind during the year. I would then step back to the doorway and hug my teacher.

Leaving school for the last time I would walk slowly back up the paved hill passing between all of the rooms where I had spent the formative years of my life. I would step up on the blacktop playground and take a moment to gaze over the area where blue ribbons were won and where neighbors came together to socialize with our unforgettable carnival. Taking a few steps forward, I would look back again and reflect on the friends I had made, the wonderful teachers who taught me so much, and the excitement of covering our heads for air raid drills and the apprehension of sugar cubes given to us to prevent polio. With a humble stride I would make my way past the jungle gym, the sawdust pit, the seesaw, slides and the meandering creek. The Patrol Boys would motion me across Wilson Avenue. From the steep incline of the street I would take one last look back at Woodmont School and, with a tear in my eye, would say thank you.

CHAPTER 14

More Than a Janitor

"Buck, Scotty, brrrrrinnnng your buckets."

IN THE late 1950s and early '60s, when that battle cry echoed over the intercom of Hillsboro High School, it was Principal John Koen summoning janitors "Buck" Buchanan and Scotty to clean up another mishap in the hallways. Buck lived on the school grounds in a house at the rear of the property, just as the janitor, Mr. Lyle, did at Parmer, and Fant Watters did at Julia Green. Janitors had thankless jobs but for the most part carried out their duties without much complaining. At least not around us kids.

School teachers in the 19th century pretty much took care of their own surroundings, particularly when only a couple of rooms made up the entire school. As the population increased and buildings enlarged, it became necessary for someone to help with the basic cleanliness and overall appearance of the schoolhouse. Janitors filled that need.

At Shawb Elementary, "Uncle" Henry Pennington, the janitor in September 1890, became more than that. He was beloved by teachers and students for keeping a pot of hot coffee over a wood stove and for warming the childrens' socks and shoes by the fire on cold, wet mornings.

During the mid-20th century, a predominant number of custodians were black and stood out vividly in our segregated white neighborhood schools. We knew their first names, nicknames and sometimes their last names. But they did more than clean up.

At Stokes Elementary in 1960, Otey Clayton maintained the facility. At Burton Elementary, a tall, thin gentleman with curly hair known as "Mater" took care of the school. Over at Julia Green School on Hobbs

Charles Cecil Gentry was the janitor at Woodmont Elementary School for many years, pictured here in the 1960s.

Road, Fant Watters was the custodian. He had a habit of cheering up kids. The portly Maude Puckett ably assisted him. When vaccinations were given throughout our school system in the '50s, sometimes reactions occurred. Similar to Hillsboro's battle cry, Principal Mathis would announce over the public address system, "Maude Puckett, bring your bucket."

After school in 1961, eighth-grader Bruce Gold was standing with Mr. Watters and other students waiting for their moms to pick them up just as the PTA mothers were entering the building for a meeting. Suddenly, a Chevy Corvair pulled along the curb and idled past everyone. The only boy in the car not baring his rear end to the crowd was the driver. A collective gasp was heard, and parents shielded their little ones as Bruce and Watters watched in shocked amazement. Finally the delinquents hit the gas and sped off. Everyone had just been "mooned." Gold recalls, "I looked at Fant, and he at me, and we laughed so hard we almost cried. This was a mess even Fant couldn't clean up."

A couple of miles away was my school, Woodmont (see previous chapter). In the early 1940s, the janitor there was a tall, quiet man nicknamed "Plez." Plez stayed in the background, was pleasant and friendly and often served as a bartender in neighboring homes for parties. Ellen (Russell) Sadler walked from her home to Woodmont with other kids, often accompanied by their dogs, a common sight in those days. In order to get Ellen's pooch and others to stay off school grounds, Plez would hurl clinkers at them. (Clinkers were basically rocks of residue from the coal furnaces that heated our homes and businesses back then.) No word if the clinkers hit their mark, but I imagine those canines got the message.

In 1948, Plez turned over the janitorial reigns of Woodmont to a special individual named Charles Cecil Gentry. Cecil was born in Lewisburg, Tenn., in 1902,

Gentry stands outside the school's auditorium in 1957.

to Charley and Nannie Gentry. Between then and 1910, when the family moved to Huntsville, Ala., his father regularly whipped him with a strap. Cecil's daughter, Cecil Charlene (Gentry) Jemison, said he told her, "That man was so mean to me." When his mom died two years later, young Cecil ran away and ended up moving in with his two cousins, one of whom, Greffie Russell, primarily raised him. He became a porter in a wholesale produce company at age 17 and eventually moved to Nashville where he married his wife, Thelma. He was hired as a chauffeur for a private family in 1930. His daughter was born in 1936 during which time he became a "Red Cap" and a porter on a Pullman car. The book "Speaking of Union Station, An Oral History of a Nashville Landmark" states, "Black men were always the Red Caps, who carried baggage to and from the trains, and the sleeping car porters.... They took great pride in keeping their cars clean and safe. Cecil Gentry was a porter on a Pullman car for many years; he observed that 'every porter was supposed to be honest. That was an honest person's job, not a crook's job, an intelligent person's job. We got along fine. It was one of the best jobs for a man in those days—I mean for a black man.'"

In the mid-1940s, he was transferred to Minnesota. With a young child now in grade school and a wife working as a nurse and missing his family greatly, he resigned and became an elevator operator at the Church Street Bennie Dillon Building in downtown Nashville, where many prominent businessmen worked. It was there in 1947 that he was recommended for and, in 1948 when his daughter was 12, took the job as the head janitor at Woodmont Grammar School on Estes Road. It was a job that not only changed Cecil's life but thousands of other children's lives for years to come.

Thelma drove him to work daily and picked him up, from 1948 to when their daughter graduated from Pearl, went to college at Howard University and returned in 1957 to go to Fisk. It was then that Jemison drove her father to Woodmont and took her nurse mother to Meharry on a daily basis.

"We only had one car, that Ford," said Jemison. "I drove my daddy to work and picked him up every day between 4:30 and 5 p.m. He always wore a tie to work because he had to look good going out there."

Cecil did what most janitors did. He spread that fragrant sweeping compound on our wooden floors and buffed them to a glistening shine. The lunch hall got an extra mopping and cleaning, for rarely did a day go by that someone didn't throw up. One kid, Paul, apparently ate something disagreeable for lunch one day, because shortly afterwards, standing at the top of the stairs on the second floor, an unsettled gastric rumbling erupted in a full "up-chuck," cascading down the staircase where Cecil was beginning his ascent. With a scowl he looked up at the youngster, whereby Paul uttered, "Sorry, Cecil." Without complaint, Cecil went about his task of cleaning up and, I might add, made sure Paul was okay.

On occasion a student would be asked to help him put up the chairs in the auditorium. Alex regarded it as a privilege. You see, Cecil had no one to help him. He was the man. He cleaned our cloak rooms, dusted the library books and wiped the shelves with one of those cloths he kept in his back pocket. He emptied those three-foot, brownish, cylindrical trash cans in the dumpster out back, and he made sure our classroom radiators were not set too high. He scraped off some of the bubble gum and melted crayons that a few mischievous kids had left on them. I knew some of those culprits pretty well…(ahem). Cheering up sick kids in the infirmary, helping the patrol ladies get us across the street and telling us goodbye (not a custodial chore) was part of what he did, all the while wearing that pleasant smile.

Let it be known he did not put up with nonsense, particularly when kids' safety or ill-mannered behavior were involved. After school in the fall of 1956, Phil Morgan decided to "fire away" with his new BB gun on some cardboard boxes in the back of the school. Cecil caught Phil in the act and in no uncertain terms, "let me know that I was not to do that around the school, plus I would have to visit the principal's office the next day."

Morgan went on to recall an earlier incident in which Cecil comforted a first-grader crying in the hall: "He knelt down in front of her, and she very quickly calmed down. Cecil had a way with kids, and he cared about them."

As a fourth-grader transferring from Eakin School to Woodmont in 1964, Austin Davis was a good athlete but a bit on the raucous side. Mark Bigham's dog, Salty, was at the center of one episode. It seems Davis and others had placed a rope over Salty and attempted to pull him in through an open window during class when a substitute teacher was in charge. Salty's disapproval led to the end of the caper. Davis was deemed to be the mastermind and not allowed to play ball that afternoon. In addition, he was made to write on the blackboard 100 times that he would "be respectful to my teacher and not make others laugh in class." Davis said he was upset and felt the punishment was unfair and the teacher was cruel. Cecil, always aware of what was going on at the school, took the youngster aside.

"He told me that I needed to learn that the punishment was not unfair and that I needed to be a man," recalled Davis, "and to quit whining like a two-year-old. He told me that I had so many blessings in life…and that I needed to be a better example for the other kids in the class rather than acting like a spoiled fool."

Cleaning the bathrooms was a part of the job that couldn't have been at the top of Mr. Gentry's list. He often discovered questionable behavior going on in there, and his prompt and respected actions spoke volumes.

In 1966, as a sixth-grader, Davis organized a peeing contest in the boy's restroom. The object was to hit the urinal from as far away as possible, starting close up. Once you missed and hit the floor you were eliminated. As you

Cecil Gentry poses with a student and patrol lady at Woodmont School in the '60s.

can imagine, this event attracted a large group of pre-pubescent kids. Davis was crowned the champ and nicknamed "PeeWall." As the boys dispersed, in came Cecil to find Davis and puddles of urine all over his freshly-mopped floor. Davis begged not to be turned in to then Principal Hill. But it was to no avail.

"Cecil told me," said Davis, "I was going to have to take my medicine like a man."

It was the worst moment of the youngster's life. Returning home, his father, a Korean War veteran, explained to him that at times during battle men had to relieve themselves in their uniforms in demanding conditions and that to disrespect the janitor by peeing on the floor was unacceptable behavior.

"I got an old-fashioned black-belt whipping before I came back to school the next day."

Davis said it was one of the hardest things he ever had to do—find Cecil the next day and apologize.

"I broke down in shame and cried to Mr. Cecil," said Davis. "I felt lower than a rat, and promised him I would try to do better. He was so wonderful to tell me that he loved me and that I was one of his Woodmont boys. He was proud of me as a man for doing something so hard as to apologize to an adult."

Davis said Cecil taught kids "to respect people, to respect property, and to never look down on someone because of their station in life."

Years later, Davis had his own "knuckleheads" in school who complained. He often cited Cecil Gentry by

Cecil Gentry and Connie (Overbey) Luttrell are pictured at the 1989 Woodmont School reunion. (Connie Luttrel)

telling those kids, "Do you know how hard it is for a grown man to come to school early every day—before others even arrive—to work hard all day picking up trash, mopping up spilled milk from lunchroom floors, cleaning toilets and never, ever complain or say one word negative about his station in life? Do you have any idea how hard it is to always be the lowest servant, to always be the person cleaning up after the party or special event—to always be the last person to leave after everyone else has gone home, and to do such a job every day with grace, pride and dignity?"

To this day Davis wonders, "Where do you find men like Mr. Cecil?"

Linda (Overbey) Parker was a very small, frail first-grader in 1953, and getting a cheerful "Hello, Little Bitty Lady" from Cecil made her feel warm and safe. From then on she got the greeting with a giggle—"there's Little Bitty Lady."

Junelle (McGaw) Barras recalled, "He seemed to know all of us by name even though we had over 500 students. Remembering Cecil makes me smile and feel good all over again, as if I were still a little girl at Woodmont. He made countless numbers of us children feel welcome and appreciated every day we were in school. How lucky we were."

The cover of the reunion program showing the school on Estes Road where today is a public park. (Connie Luttrell)

According to Kathy (Hedrick) Bass, she and Cecil had a special hand-shake that occurred when she would turn in her tray at the window after lunch. Cecil always helped out Mrs. McClure during lunch.

"He would wipe his hand off on his pants and shake my hand," said Bass. "He never failed to do this. He was such a sweet man."

His help unloading parents' cars for the paper and coat-hanger drives did not go unnoticed by Mary Louise (Frist) Barfield.

"My mother always carried on a conversation with him," said Barfield, "remarking how fine he was and how hard he worked. He was a great example for us. Many life lessons were learned from him. He taught us what it meant to give of oneself. Cecil was a true gentleman."

Kathy (Thweatt) Morton said Cecil knew everyone's name and had a smile for each student. His willingness to talk, give advice and be kind made him the favorite of all the staff.

Connie (Overbey) Luttrell said he referred to all the girls as "pretty little ladies."

"Regardless of his race, job position, etc., we were all friends with Cecil," said Luttrell. "Long remembered and admired."

Mary Dale (Trabue) Fitzgerald said, "When school zones changed in 1957 and I came to Woodmont from Julia Green as a sixth-grader, everyone was welcoming. But the person who greeted me every morning and melted away my fears and apprehension as a newcomer and called me by name was Cecil. He had a great smile and remarkable memory. Cecil Gentry was a major contributor to that very special, caring place."

Student Emily (Glasgow) Bruno: "I loved him."

Enough said.

In 1966, Cecil's wife, Thelma, died, and Mr. Garriott, his longtime friend and principal, left to go to Hillwood. Cecil retired the following year. He continued to do parties, weddings (my sister's included) and the like for many more years for the parents of the children he had come to know and love while at that neighborhood school on Estes Road.

At the Woodmont School reunion in 1989, with hundreds in attendance, Cecil Gentry was the one who got the most attention. His contagious smile and name recognition had not waned a bit. He knew me right off the bat. Some of my marginal behavior probably left a mark.

His only school custodial job was there at an all-white, upper-middle-class, segregated school during a time of racial unrest. I wondered what his feelings were about tending to white kids and parents at our school during that period. I asked his daughter if he ever complained or said anything about working for people like that. She quickly and emphatically said with a watery eye, "He didn't fool with all that stuff. That man loved that school. Those were his boys and girls. You can't mention Cecil without saying Woodmont."

Cecil Charles Gentry died in 1993 at 91 years of age. Janelle (Hood) Haseman, a student at Woodmont from 1952 to 1960, put it this way: "Whenever I think of Woodmont, I envision a big white building with Cecil Gentry superimposed on it. His smile and charisma were infectious. We were blessed to have him in our lives."

I only wish us kids had told him how much he meant to us when he was still around. I think he knew that. If not, he for certain knows now.

CHAPTER 15

Cupid's Arrow

Cupid draw back your bow
And let your arrow go
Straight to my lover's heart for me, for me
Cupid please hear my cry
And let your arrow fly
Straight to my lover's heart, for me.
—Sam Cooke, "Cupid" (1961)

MY FIRST real interaction with the opposite sex began in the first grade with the celebration of Valentine's Day, Feb. 14, 1954. It was the day each child was to bring Valentine cards to school to pass out to other friends, in essence letting them know you liked them. It did not matter at age 7 or 8 if you gave them to a boy or a girl.

These little red-and-white cards came in cut-out form or were perforated for easy removal, usually from notebook pages. You could buy them individually at your neighborhood Rexall drug store. You, or your mom, would cut or punch out each one and write your name on it and who it was for. They were mostly one-dimensional pictures, such as a Cupid inside a heart with a bow and arrow and an inscription "Be my Valentine."

They were placed in white envelopes and usually carried to school in your back pack. I carried mine in my tin Hopalong Cassidy lunch box. Once at school each child had a cardboard box lined up on the windowsill beside the radiators. The boxes were decorated with hearts and doilies and had a slot in the top for you to drop the greeting into.

It wasn't a big deal at first, but as I moved into the second and third grades

This World War II-era card was given to Bernice Link. Below is a circa 1952 Valentine of Mary De Heckman Elliston. (Nashville Metro Archives)

pressure mounted to see how many I could get, especially from girls. It basically turned into a popularity contest. And by the way, when the fourth, fifth and sixth grades rolled around, I gave very few to other boys.

Another thing about these cards, you could almost cite the year of the greeting by what was depicted on the front. My older sisters' cards probably had a military motif. Switchboard operators, locomotives, washtubs and the like were all used to come up with a clever theme. Some of the better ones even had moving parts and were three-dimensional.

A third-century priest named Valentine started all of this. Seems an evil emperor named Claudius II decided that single men made better fighters than married ones, so he outlawed marriage. Valentine determined this was an injustice and performed secret marriages for love-struck couples. You can guess the rest—Claudius executed him. One story goes that while imprisoned the priest became enamored with the jailer's daughter and sent her what has argu-ably been called the first Valentine, stating to her, "From your Valentine"—a saying that is today typical on most cards on February 14th. That date during the Middle Ages in France and England was widely accepted as the beginning of the mating season for birds.

I am not sure about the birds, but mating for humans was not sea-sonal, especially during adolescence and early adulthood, and not always on

Valentine's Day.

As far as the tradition of exchanging letters and cards, we have a lady named Esther Howland (Mother of the Valentine) to thank. She began mass-producing colorful cards from lace, ribbons and pictures in the 1840s.

Above is a circa 1938 Valentine card of Doris Hutton Holt. Below, a circa 1940 Valentine card of Mary De Heckman Elliston. (Nashville Metro Archives)

For us school kids, Valentine cards became more pertinent with each grade. You were determined by others to have a boyfriend or girlfriend if you gave only a few out and then sat beside that classmate on pur-

pose, in the lunch hall or in assembly, on a regular basis. Word spread that "Ed loves Susan" or "Bruce likes Nancy," or something like that. Teasing usually followed with the biting words spouted out in verse form: "Bill and Mary sitting in a tree, K-I-S-S-I-N-G...."

There wasn't much kissing going on until the hormones started to elevate, along about age 11 or 12. In 1957 in the fourth grade I made a "date" with a Woodmont cutie but inexplicably failed to follow through. It was not forgotten. As related to me later, "I was all dressed up with nowhere to go." No Valentine card from her that year. By the time the seventh and eighth grades came around, the game of Spin the Bottle shed new light on the opposite sex. Ages 13 through 16 were in a class of their own.

Most "dates" in late grade school required the watchful eye of suspicious

parents. Your every move
while in the car was monitored, limiting the exchanges
to clandestine maneuvers.
Social functions were a little
different, particularly if the
parents were not home.

During 1959–1960, I was
invited to a Valentine party
hosted by a girl I knew on
West End Avenue. The mov-
ie at the Belle Meade Theater
just down the road was "Ten
Thousand Bedrooms," billed
as "Great for grownups." Not
what our folks wanted us to

Shadow dancers from the 1959 Hillsboro High School annual. (Nashville Metro Archives)

see, so that option was out, leaving the party as my only alternative.

I got all spruced up, via my mother. Madras shirt and pressed pants, blaz-
er, fresh hair cut with just a dab of Vitalis, some Butch Wax, a little Aqua
Velva aftershave, and I was set. No Clearasil needed, yet. I did refuse to bring
flowers, although a Valentine special of corsages, roses and plants ranged from
$3 to $10 at Emma's.

The parents directed us into a well-lit den and set out various non-alco-
holic drinks for the affair. Roy Orbison and the Everly Brothers were being
spun on the hi-fi. I remember taking a seat in a large straight-back cushioned
chair when a young lady friend decided to sit with (or on) me and was not
going to get up. Quite the advanced move. Finally the soft drink she had
consumed earlier necessitated a trip upstairs to the rest room. Another girl,
in the clutches of a classmate, leaned over to me and said, "[Name withheld
to protect the guilty] wants to make out with you if you will kiss her."

Not being clueless, I already had an idea that is what she wanted. I leaned
over and said, "I wouldn't mind, but she must have eaten an entire onion
earlier in the day. Her breath is atrocious."

Who knows how that was conveyed, but a bathroom break gave me the opportunity to move freely about the surroundings. Never again did I sit in one place too long.

"Make-out parties," as we called them, from the 1950s through the '60s were personified by the long-playing records and 45s we put on the hi-fi. In 1960 I spent a Friday night out at a friend's home. He was not known for shyness regarding the opposite sex. He invited 10 of us to a "get-together," five of each gender, and we assembled in his parents' den at the far reaches of his house. The parents, chaperones in name only, failed to make an appearance, which encouraged "misbehavior." The record player was set and no more than six sitting areas were strewn about. Obviously some doubling-up was required. It was an evening of "petting," but nothing beyond that (I think). Who knows with whom it was you slow danced, for the lighting was non-existent. I do believe it was a female, however. Ray Charles would have felt right at home. The hugs and kisses were not in short supply, all enhanced by Johnny Mathis, who, in 1956, opted to make his first recordings rather than accept an offer to try out for the USA Olympic team as a high jumper. That decision led us youths to years of decadent behavior. That night his "Twelfth of Never," "Wonderful Wonderful," "Chances Are," "When Sunny Gets Blue" and "It's Not for Me to Say" seemed to recycle every 30 minutes, broken up only by the Fleetwoods' "Mr. Blue" and "Come Softly to Me."

These make-out parties occurred all over town in dimly-lit dens, basements and isolated rooms of family homes. I know previous generations participated in such teen activities, just with different songs. We played those '50s, "kissy-face" numbers that our predecessors listened to as well. Tommy Edwards' tune of "It's All in the Game" sounded just like Johnny Mathis. Some of the songs that put us youngsters "in the mood" included the 1961 ballad by Gene Pitney titled "Town Without Pity." There were the Platters recordings of "The Great Pretender" and "Only You." Others that caused lipstick smears and "passion marks" (superficial bruising on the side of the neck caused by sucking, usually dime-sized but could vary in diameter and number) that we proudly displayed were "In the Still of the Night," "16 Candles," "Since I Don't Have You," "You Belong to Me," "Oh What a Night" by the Dells, "Silhouettes," "Earth Angel," and Percy Faith's "A Summer Place."

All of these caused testosterone levels to rise during slow dancing. Slow

A favorite record album of the author that "enhanced the hugs and kisses."

dancing was nothing more than a standing hug for the duration of a song, at least when I was involved. A couple that was really "wrapped up" in a slow dance, whether at a combo or school function, usually prompted this comment from onlookers: "Guess somebody is gonna get some tonight." However engrossed you became, you dared not let your date know of just how much the occasion had "peaked your interest." That would be a party killer, at least until your prime teenage years when tomfoolery ran wild.

Those early pre-driving years were just warm-ups to the main events to come. Once 16, we no longer had to be dropped off and picked up by our parents from these social affairs and required to endure a line of questioning on the way home, some of which would make Sergeant Joe Friday of "Dragnet" proud. Our answers were often misleading at best. "Listening to records" was the standard reply. Once a teen could drive, all bets were off. With no parental guidance, proper moral behavior was defined by two teenagers in the throes of a life change (not a parent's dream).

Most of us dated and had girl- or boyfriends, some of whom were "snowed" over the other (a term meaning you were in the "puppy love mode" and the object of your affection could do no wrong). Others just kind of matriculated along through school. For those of us who did date, those parties ramped up a notch and often only included you and your current date for the evening. Music remained the catalyst for vanishing inhibitions.

We listened to tunes on the radio while cruising in cars with reclining seats…and no seat belts (making it especially easy for your sweetie to slide over next to you). We parked on Nine Mile Hill and atop Laurel Ridge.

We snuggled on a blanket in Percy Warner Park or on a desolate road near Radnor Lake under the stars. We put on those records while caressing in darkened rooms, on den sofas…and in other places.

We used to say, "That's our song," when a certain one was played. Some of those memory-makers included Sunny and the Sunglows' "Talk to Me," Lenny Welch's "Since I Fell for You," Barbara Lewis' "Baby I'm Yours," Smokey Robinson's "Tracks of My Tears," and "My Girl" by the Temptations. There were "You Don't Have to Be a Baby to Cry" by the Caravelles, "Gee Whiz" by Carla Thomas, "I Only Have Eyes for You" by The Flamingos, "Angel Baby" by Rosie and the Originals, "Tonight's the Night" by the Shirells, "Whispering" by April Stevens and Nino Tempo, and "I'm Leaving It Up to You" by Dale and Grace. Mood-enhancers included Mathis and Connie Francis, locals Ronnie and the Daytonas ("Sandy") and songs by the Bobbys (Vinton, Rydell and Vee), Dick and Dee Dee, and the Righteous Brothers. "So Much in Love" by The Tymes, "Our Day Will Come" by Ruby and the Romantics, "Don't Worry Baby" by the Beach Boys, "Chapel of Love" by The Dixie Cups, "Groovin" by Young Rascals, "At Last" by Etta James, and "Sleep Walk" by Santo and Johnny often caused a substantial amount of disrobement and wandering hands.

The simple Valentine cards we passed out in the first grade and the songs that played when we started "noticing" the opposite sex were special. We all had different experiences, some good, some not so much, and some a little of both. Cupid's arrow was not always on target. Those songs of the past can be painful, but they can also transport us to a time many years ago…back to what it felt like to be young, carefree and living in the moment.

So if you get to feeling down and out, do what I sometimes do—load up the hi-fi with those old vinyls, pour yourself a drink, sit back and once again "Be Young, Be Foolish, Be Happy." It might take you to a place you haven't been in a while…a place you just might want to revisit time and again.

CHAPTER 16

Baseball in My Youth

M Y GRANDMOTHER told my mom that all she had to do was give my dad a ball and he would be happy. That proved to be true as he became a great athlete in many sports, all involving a ball of some kind.

As far back as I can remember, that remark was passed down about me. Although I never achieved the accolades of my father, I was nonetheless enamored with the objects.

Baseball was particularly appealing because it was played in warm weather and allowed for outdoor activity. Swinging one of those large Louisville Slugger bats, autographed by Babe Ruth or Mickey Mantle, gave one the feeling of stardom.

The Babe was a bit before my

The author prepares to hit a baseball in 1950 at the age of 3.

time; Mickey was my guy. Theresa Brewer even wrote a song about him. An impressive figure, he sported muscles and swung the bat from either side, producing homer after homer.

When my coordination was sufficient enough to warrant contact with a baseball, my dad would throw to me across the street in a large open space

A sandlot baseball game is played on Herbert's Field circa March 1956. (Nashville Metro Archives, Paul Clements Collection)

called Herbert's Field. He had an old raggedy bag full of balls of all shades of white. Many had been painted with white shoe polish to make them more visible. He would pitch to me, and I would strike those leather spheres one after another until all were gone from his cache. At that point we would both run to gather them up and start the process all over again. I hit some; I missed some. Unfortunately, all that practice never materialized into a major league star, just a well-known grade schooler.

In 1953 the "Game of the Week" began airing on ABC television and later on CBS. It was sponsored by Falstaff beer, which I later discovered tasted a little like the smell that came from a specimen one would produce for an annual physical. Famed St. Louis pitcher (and former Park Avenue Elementary, Cohn High and Hume-Fogg student) Johnny Beasley later became the local distributor. So now into our homes on Saturdays, as part of the "Game," came a larger-than-life, 300-pound, Stetson-hat-and-string-tie-wearing, Hall-of-Fame-pitcher-turned-announcer Dizzy Dean. His academic career ended in the second grade, and as ole Diz said: "And I wasn't so good in first either." When he was inducted into the Hall of Fame as a player he said: "The good Lord was good to me. He gave me a strong body, a good right arm, and a weak mind." His use of our language became a hit with youngsters and homespun folks alike, but he caused English teachers to wince at his every word. During slow periods of the game he would often serenade fellow play-by-play man Buddy Blattner and later Pee Wee Reese with his rendition

of "Wabash Cannonball." According to Dizzy: a player "slud into third," bat-
ters "swang," pitchers "throwed" and runners returned to "their respectable
bases." He called a pop fly a "can of corn." When an argument with an umpire
took place Dean once said it was "like argyin' with a stump. Maybe you city
folks don't know what a stump is. It's somethin' a tree has been cut down off
of." He called everyone "pod-nuh." The head of CBS Sports Bill McPhail
said: "Watching Dizzy Dean was an absolute religion." I was hooked along
with millions of other citizens.

In the mid- to late 1950s I began to collect baseball cards. Having discovered a newfound freedom with bicycles, several of us neighborhood boys
would make regular trips the mile or so down to Moon Drugs to buy several
packs of Topps baseball cards. They were usually five cards for 5 cents and had
that wonderful-tasting, flat, powdery piece of bubble gum wrapped up with
them. Card collecting became an obsession. I especially liked the backs of
those cards with the cartoon-like drawings of past achievements of featured
players. There was always something to say regardless how unknown that
individual was.

We traded duplicate cards with other kids who had extras of those we
wanted. Everyone wanted Willie Mays, Mickey Mantle, Sandy Koufax and
all the big stars. I had several of those, but what I seemed to get the most of
was what they called "common cards." Minnie Minoso, Preacher Roe, Rip
Repulski and Coot Veal were just a few. On the back of Coot's 1959 card it
read: "He came to the Tigers on July 30, 1958, and became a full-fledged Major
Leaguer immediately." I managed to get the cards of some of the Nashville
Vols who made it to the big leagues, such as Bob Lennon, who hit 64 home
runs in 1954 for Nashville, and catcher Dutch Dotterer, who played for the
Cincinnati Redlegs. The back of his card said: "Dutch holds the unique dis-
tinction of having caught a ball dropped from a helicopter"—inside information every kid wanted to know. The majority of my collection either wound
up glued onto my bedroom wall or used to make my bike sound like a motorcycle. I would grab my mother's wooden clothes pins from our clothesline and
attach baseball cards to the wire spokes on my bike. Combined with balloons,
those common cards made quite an impressive sound.

Organizing games came easy to me for some reason. I had the ability to

A Knothole game in 1958, between Jersey Farms Milk and the Brookmeade Tigers, is played at Elmington Park in front of West End High School. The author is the pitcher. West End Church of Christ is in the background. (Nashville Metro Archives, Paul Clements Collection)

corral enough neighborhood kids on hot days to form two baseball teams and to have them gather in a nearby field for an afternoon of fun. Rules differed according to the field and number of players participating. For instance, you could not hit to one of the outfields or only hit to the third base side because we did not have enough kids to play every position. Stealing was not allowed, but we got around that by getting into "rundowns." In the major leagues a runner got caught between two bases and was thrown out immediately, but in our case the runner usually made it an error-filled home run as throwing mishaps were the norm.

Bases were often an old t-shirt, towel or piece of wood, which made sliding perilous at times. Our ball gloves, particularly new ones, were often greased with neatsfoot oil. To form a pocket in the glove we placed a baseball in the center then tied the glove into a closed position with string. The pocket provided us with the best opportunity to catch.

There were sandlots all over town where pickup games occurred. Each yard, field or open lot was deemed a place to play, and most every one was in bike-riding distance of home. Each place had its own characteristics.

In the early 1950s, Phillip Wright played at the old Centenary Community Center in North Nashville with neighborhood kids.

On my side of town there were many. Elmington Park in front of West High School even had bleachers. Over at Herbert's Field, tucked behind Lynnbrook, Westmont and Cantrell, there was always a game. They even had a wooden backstop constructed there. Should you slug one past one of the outfielders it would roll

The front and back of the 1956 Topps card for Bob Lennon, a former Nashville Vols player turned major leaguer.

forever, almost always assuring one of a home run. There was the Thackston lot on Estes Road featuring, a creek that ran behind first base. Rubber balls had to be used there.

Rose bushes that were not to be disturbed came into play at the Kuhn's at the corner of Snead and Trimble. Jim Barr organized that game. According to Tom Bailey: "You could always find a game in the Clarks' front yard on Wayland. Those games were organized by David Gennett and featured Buddy Bracey, Barney Ross, and four or five Clark brothers. There was also Stocky and Tucky, who personified their names. That venue featured a huge creek that ran through the outfield, spawning all sorts of intricate ground rules that had to be agreed on before each game."

On Skyline Drive around Bill Jordon's home yard, many kids from Julia

Green participated in games, and I am told the choosing of teams was quite contentious at times.

Gid Wade hosted games just down from the Clark lot. Bailey recalls: "Baseball card trading was also rife at Gid's, and his mother also fed us all lunch or dinner so that we could resume the marathon games we played there. There was a game on Esteswood in John Drury's front yard. The field was lousy—there were a lot of spindly trees you had to play the ball off of—but the company was just fine. There was also a game near the Chapmans' on Copeland. I can't remember exactly where we played, but with the Chapmans in the game, it was always lively, if not downright fractious."

On Lynnbrook Road two blocks from my house, the Tompkins had a large back yard/field that had been fenced in. This gave us the feeling of being in a major-league park. Clifton Sobel seemed to relish hitting homers over the fence and through the glass sliding door and windows in the Huggins home next door. The last shot was a monstrous blow that disappeared over the carport eventually creating the discomforting sound of shattering glass. Shortly thereafter "Skinny" (Mr. Huggins) came out with the ball in his hand as we scattered from the area.

Most of the kids who played in those lots also played Knothole, the equivalent of Little League. My dad coached several of us Woodmont kids with the help of sponsor Clyde Moon of Moon Drugs. That was our name. In 1958 it was Jersey Farms Milk, and you might say we gave our best, which basically means we did not win much. I was often the pitcher, sporting an ERA (earned run average) slightly more than my age (11). We did manage to win two games that year but lost six. Our overall play was much like spoiled Jersey Farms Milk tasted—not good. Knothole was big in those days, with the local papers often printing scores of the games.

In 1961, at age 14, I went to stay a couple of days with my sister and my brother-in-law, who was interning in Cincinnati. Through their benevolence I was presented with a ticket to see the Redlegs play the San Francisco Giants—my first major league game in person. One of my baseball idols, Willie "the Say Hey Kid" Mays, was in the line-up for the Giants. The Treniers in 1955 even sang a song about him:

He runs the bases like a choo-choo train
Swings around second like an aeroplane
His cap flies off when he passes third
And he heads home like an eagle bird.
Say Hey, say who?
Say Willie, Swinging at the plate
Say Hey, say who?
Say Willie, That Giants kid is great

Never mind Frank Robinson, Vada Pinson and the hometown stars—I was excited to see Willie. The game was played at Crosley Field, reminiscent somewhat of Sulphur Dell in Nashville. After visiting the concession area and purchasing an A&W root beer in one of those megaphone containers, I returned to my seat along the first-base side some 20 rows from the field.

From there I saw Willie Mays up at bat, and I was glued to his every move. I thought, "Maybe he will foul one off in my direction." Sure enough he hit a high foul ball, and the more it traveled the more it came towards me. I finally realized I had a play on it. Emptying my root beer I hoisted the container skyward just as the ball came down. It grazed the top of my cup, hit the concrete walk directly behind me and bounded some 20 feet in the air, coming down to a throng of other fans. After a brief skirmish, some vulgarities and a few scrapes, some lucky adult came out of the pile with the prize: a major league baseball off the bat of Willie Mays. For me, I was left with what might have been and an empty root-beer megaphone.

There are no more Dizzys, Willies and Mickeys, and the "Game of the Week" turned into games of the day. The homes and street corners with big yards, fields used for sandlot games, and neighborhood drug stores where we used to ride our bikes to buy cards, have all disappeared. However, the friends we made and relationships formed in those open areas and lots have not gone away. It is something all kids who played in those days should treasure. Count me as one who does.

CHAPTER 17

Man's Best Friend

MY FAVORITE companion for the first several years of life had four legs and barked. His name was Red—a red Irish Cocker Spaniel who loved life, kids and mischief. He was in mid-life form and I was not quite 3 when we became best friends in 1949. He followed me when I was pushed around in my Taylor Tot stroller, licked me when I would fall down, and took many a ride in my Radio Flyer wagon attached to my tricycle. He even rode on my American Flyer sled during the blizzard of 1951. He was an outside dog and roamed free, as did most dogs of that era. Red's activities included attacking the Haury's chickens, harassing the Sebelius cats, digging in flower beds and disrupting sandlot baseball and football events across the street at Herbert's field.

When I got older he followed me to grade school and waited for my return. He loved a good roll on his back in the leaves and lusted after the opposite sex (not unlike us boys eventually would). Bathing in an old washtub in the back yard or in the double

The author pets his first dog, Red, in 1948.

The author sits atop Rags in 1953.

sink we had in the basement was not one of his favorite activities. He showed his displeasure by shaking the suds and water off of his drenched sandy-red hair. An occasional upchuck on the porch never sat well with my mother, nor did his yapping at our parakeet, Buzzy, who was caged in our den. He would let me pull his ears, lie on his back, and brush out the cockleburs he had acquired while carousing the neighborhood.

Since that time canines of varying descriptions and colors have been part of my existence. My belief is that the famous WWI German-shepherd hero Rin-Tin-Tin, or "Rinty" as he was affectionately called, and the Little Rascals American pit bull with the circled eye, Petey, both started a dog boom when those radio shows became television syndications in the 1950s. (Petey was truly "Hollywood"; I learned later in life that make-up artist Max Factor applied Petey's trademark ring.)

Dog dining in our home was relegated to the pantry, to beside the stove, or outside. My mom used to be appalled when my paternal grandmother would hold her plate down for a thorough licking by man's best friend. Scraps were routinely given, but the ever-popular Ken-L Ration canned food was big in our household. Our dogs didn't care for Pard; I think the name made them ill. At one time or another we tried Hills, Gro-Pup, Red Heart and even Ken-L-Kan. Dog food companies became quite prevalent with Gravy Train and those hamburger-resembling patties called Gainesburgers. Competition was fierce in 1963 as Friskies offered an authentic Indian head dress for just $3.50 with proof of purchase, playing off of the Walt Disney movie "Savage Sam." Canned food was huge prior to WWII but tailed off during the war as horses were no longer needed as much and the demand for tin waned, clearing the way for the dry variety.

Types and names of dogs reflected the times. I had a few collies, mainly because of the television series "Lassie." "Trouble with Father," starring Stu Erwin, prompted one to be named Stu. He was the temperamental dog, and with all the kids who played in our yard, my folks felt he needed to be put in a pen. One afternoon when let out, he inexplicably sank his teeth into Wilton Burnett's right buttock while he bent over to get a drink out of our hose pipe. I think Stu was moved to the country after that.

I named another collie Ike, after our president Dwight Eisenhower, whose slogan was "I Like Ike." Distemper took that dog's life. It was a sad time.

Paul Clements and John Woods adopted two mix breeds from Thayer Hospital on White Bridge Road during this time. John named his Sluggo from the comic strip, and Paul labeled his Zorro after the TV show that was airing at the time. A fellow grade-school neighbor, Ricky Chambers, went for the military tag and called his dog Rommel.

A Great Dane that lived two blocks away from me was called Rags by the Ragland family and was a regular visitor to my yard. He used to let me

The author plays with his dog Topper in 1954.

go for a ride on his back.
Great Danes were popular,
especially in the 1960 car-
toons "Scooby-Doo" and
"The Jetsons," featuring
Astro.

One of my favorite TV
programs was "Topper." It
aired in the mid-1950s and
featured a huge St. Bernard
named Neil. The show was
about Cosmo Topper, the
main character, trying to
coexist with his energetic
wife, Henrietta. About
that time I acquired a spotted beagle-cocker mix and
named him Topper. My
neighbor, Alex, bought his
first and only small mutt

Carolyn Henderson gives Kris a treat in 1968 while Tom was in Vietnam.

and called her, fittingly, Henrietta.

Topper slept in our basement and was my constant companion for several
years, until we had a torrential rain event. As fate would have it my mom
opened the door that led down to Topper's sleeping quarters just as he whizzed
by, and down the steps he went. We didn't know that water had flooded the
entire basement. Topper took a leap, hit the water, then exited quickly. The
next day he disappeared, never to be seen again.

Shortly thereafter Henrietta failed to come home; we found her in a
ditch off of Bowling Avenue, an apparent victim of a hit-and-run. Alex and
I buried her in his back yard, tied two sticks together for a cross, spread some
bricks over the grave, and said a few words before solemnly walking away.

In the '50s and '60s dogs were featured not only in TV shows and
comic books but in song, movies, and advertisements as well. Scotties were
big in whiskey ads while Dalmatians were featured in Texaco Oil spots

wearing fire chief hats. "101 Dalmatians" in 1961 added to their allure.

The Selph family named their small dachshund Gidget from the movie by the same name. Gidget's daily exercise routine was making continuous circles in the kitchen running behind appliances while Mr. Selph clapped his hands. Friend Mary Beth Oliver went for the name Buddy, as their mix was a friend to all. My

Carolyn reads a magazine to their son, Todd, in the company of their dog Bogey in 1971.

aunt and uncle, the Mintons, had on their farm a cow-wrangling mix breed named Elvis.

The movie "The Shaggy Dog" and the tearjerker "Old Yeller" increased pooch ownership and further solidified the bond between a kid and his dog. Dog appeal was also enhanced by the TV series "Sgt. Preston of the Yukon" and the dog King. Patti Page's recording of "How Much Is That Doggy in the Window" hit No. 1 in 1953, no doubt boosting business at Jones Pet Store in the Belmont area. And the 1963 recording "Walking the Dog" by Rufus Thomas enabled hormone-laden teens to simulate animal instincts on the dance floor.

In the late 1950s I was given a blond cocker for Christmas. I named him Kris for the mythical holiday figure Kris Kringle. Kris became my mother and father's last dog at home when I married in 1967.

During my courting years I would occasionally bring a date home because of the proximity of our semi-detached playroom from the main part of our house. I have often thought my folks played a role in what I called "absentee chaperoning." Suspicion continues to this day that Kris was fed an evening buffet of highly-seasoned pork giblets, four-way chili and leftover lasagna, and

then sent out to our get-
away just minutes before
my date and I would arrive.
Sitting on our sofa with
romantic music playing
in the background on the
hi-fi and a good-looking
lass snuggling close was a
much-anticipated event.
Unfortunately another
event often took place on
the floor just behind the
couch. Kris would be in his
favorite spot and, with no
regard for decency, would
let loose a clothes-fading,
eye-watering, gaseous
emission that would engulf
the entire area. Right on

The author plays Frisbee with his dog Bogey in 1970.

cue my father would suddenly appear spraying a large container of fruity-
scented Glade, choking both the dog and us. The combination of odors generally caused testosterone levels to recede dramatically and required further
amorous advances to be realized at another location.

Ironically, in 1969, my wife and I regularly were called to pick up Kris
several blocks away, being told by neighbors that he and a female were up to
no good. His romance-ending fumes evidently had no effect on his love life.

In 1969 my brother-in-law gave my wife, Carolyn, and me a puppy
he found at Harpeth Hills Golf Course, just as we were about to move to
Memphis. We named him Bogey. He was our first dog as a couple and became
part of us for almost two decades. He loved to catch a Frisbee after running
hundreds of yards. He slept vigilantly on our bed and sat in our laps for comfort and protected us from strangers. He allowed us to take in strays without
putting up a fight and regularly tolerated the three-hour drive from Memphis
to Nashville, often sharing the backseat of our Volkswagon (see Chapter 12).

When our first son, Todd, was born, Bogey was relegated to second-tier status. He accepted it, protected him, and later on did the same for our other kids, until his kidneys failed at the age of 19.

From the 1940s through the 1960s, kids' dogs generally had an entire neighborhood as their exercise area. They were part of the surroundings. It was common for them to follow us to football practice, carnivals and community events, and run along beside our bicycles in route to baseball or softball games. They followed and waited for us patiently at our grade schools, ran across vacant lots and sprinted across unfenced back yards and through holes in hedges. They rode in our non-air conditioned cars and went to work with parents.

Times changed as annexation occurred, leash laws were enacted and neighborhood schools vanished. Vacant lots disappeared and were sold and divided for high-end homes. Kids walking or riding their bikes to nearby fields ended and neighbors began to fence in their yards.

Not only had kids' lives changed but our dogs had as well.

To paraphrase Jimmy Stewart's poem about his dog:

> *There are nights I think I can feel him*
> *crawl up on our bed,*
> *Lie between us and I would pat*
> *his head.*
> *I think at times I can feel his stare*
> *And reach out my hand to stroke his hair,*
> *Only to realize he's not there.*
> *O how I wish that wasn't to be*
> *For I miss my best friend Red, Kris,*
> *and especially,*
> *Our first one as a couple,*
> *named Bogey.*

CHAPTER 18

The Monsters and
Dr. Lucifer

MONOGRAM PICTURES released one of the great horror films of all time in 1948, entitled "The Bowery Boys Meet Frankenstein." In the mid-1950s my father took a bunch of us neighborhood kids to see it at the now-gone Belmont Theater on 21st Avenue in Hillsboro Village. The goof-ball Bowery Boy, Sach (Huntz Hall), had his mind, such as it was, transplanted with the monster's brain. On another occasion we saw an equally comedic fright film at a matinee showing in the same venue, "Bud Abbott and Lou Costello Meet Frankenstein." Shrieks and laughter abounded in that historic cinema as hundreds of youngsters spilled popcorn and candy throughout the aisles.

The original classic horror movie "Frankenstein," staring Boris Karloff, was released by Universal Studios in 1931. It was not until the mid-1950s re-release that I saw it for the first time at the Princess Theater (later Crescent) downtown on Church Street by the L&C Tower. I was a mere child around the age of 10 when I went with a friend. It scared me to death. I remember getting up from my seat and retreating back up the aisle to the lobby just so I could see some people in the daylight and escape Karloff's clutches. Nightmares followed, which prompted my parents to explain that everyone I saw in the movie was acting. That was my first real foray into the world of horror.

Growing up in the Atomic Age had its drawbacks. The first atom bomb test in 1945 started it all, and the war-ending attack on Japan displayed the devastating catastrophe it could cause. Our grade-school classrooms became practice zones in case one was dropped on our city. The familiar position of heads down on your desk is still a vivid memory. However, there were some pluses, particularly if you enjoyed scary-monster and sci-fi picture shows.

Throughout the 1950s and into the 1960s science-fiction, monster and space movies abounded, albeit most were of the C-grade variety. On Oct. 23, 1959, the Nashville Banner headline read "Rocket Research Speed-Up Planned." Theaters and the relatively-new medium of television capitalized on the fears and began showing films exaggerating the after-effects of an atomic holocaust and outer space invasions. "The Blob," "Battle in Outer Space," and "The Amazing Colossal Man" come to mind.

In the fall of 1958, WSIX-TV Channel 8 decided to liven up Friday nights by launching a program called "Shock Theater," which initially featured mostly horror classics from Universal Studios. (I remember anticipating the opening of those movies with the airplane circling a globe.) The TV program originally aired at 10:15 p.m. Friday right after "NewsScope" with Hudley Crockett. Ken Bramming, already recognized for his broadcast voice and personality, was chosen to introduce the movies. Classics such

"Bud Abbott & Lou Costello Meet Frankenstein" (1948) and other films were enjoyed by the author as a kid in Nashville theaters. Such fare also aired on the local TV program "Shock Theater."

as "Frankenstein," "Dracula" with Bela Lugosi, the Lon Chaney "Wolfman" series, and my favorite, "Son of Frankenstein" starring Basil Rathbone, made up the feature list. The Sherlock Holmes and Mr. Moto mysteries were also part of the fare.

Dr. Lucifur (Ken Bramming) as he appeared in the intro to his TV program "Shock Theater." Notice the "Mystic Circle" effect. (Jeff Thompson)

Eventually the show moved to 10:30 p.m. on Saturday nights. In his article "Dr. Lucifur: Nashville TV's Tasteful Transylvanian," historian Jeff Thompson details the show's history. He quotes Bramming as saying, "We knew we would get a young audience on those nights. We were aiming for the 10- to 14-year-olds, but their parents ended up watching the show with them and liking it as much as the kids!"

I was in the crosshairs of that demographic and contributed to the show's No. 1 rating for that time slot on those nights between 1958 and 1962. According to Bramming, "Shock Theater" even beat out the "Tonight Show" with Jack Paar during that period. Much of that jump came from Bramming's idea to introduce a macabre Master of Ceremonies, live skits during breaks in the evening's feature, and some Dave Brubek jazz tunes to placate the adults.

"Shock" became almost a ritual, as several neighborhood kids would gravitate to my home and enter into our large, isolated playroom from our backyard. It was separated from the rest of our house by a long hallway. We would sit up in front of our portable TV set, the kind with the built-in rabbit-ear antennas.

Usually I, Dave, Sam and others would wait anxiously for the introduction from Dr. Lucifur. On the small, black-and-white screen, an ominous-looking

figure would material-
ize out of the darkness
to cheesy, funeralesque
organ music. The figure
was a man sporting an eye
patch, a cigarette holder,
a thin, dark mustache and
slicked-back hair. Wearing
a tuxedo with a white
tie, black tails and a long
black cape of some kind,
his entrance was enhanced
by a spinning circle superimposed on the television
screen. It was called the
"Mystic Circle." A layer of
fog produced by a dry-ice
machine swirled around
as the Doctor stood in the
light of a lamppost. This
imposing figure urged all
of us to come with him on

Ken Bramming on the "Shock Theater" set called the Purple Grotto, which featured a door stained with bloody handprints. (Jeff Thompson)

"these journeys into the worlds of mystery, the supernatural, fantasy, and the world beyond."

Often in the background one could see the Purple Grotto, one of the more famous sets, which featured a door covered in bloody handprints.

Dr. Lucifur spoke in a dialect reminiscent of Bela Lugosi in the original "Dracula" movie and somewhat resembled famed horror actor Vincent Price. Dr. Lucifur's chilling postscript to each presentation was, "Good night and pleasant dreams!" followed by a ghoulish laugh. Dr. Lucifur gained such popu-larity that he appeared at several downtown department stores during those years. According to Thompson, Bramming later said: "And the kids climbed all over me."

As I got a little older I had been conditioned, through my experience

"*Missile to the Moon*" (1958)

with Frankenstein, to take these films and actors for what they were—actors. Dr. Lucifur, I knew, was only Ken Bramming in make-up, but he was still a specter and not easily forgotten. We kids eventually became highly entertained by the whole proceedings, especially when the skits took place. According to Thompson, Bramming used a high-schooler at the time named Corky Savely who regularly appeared as Granny Gruesome, Frantic Freddy the Hipster and Cyril Songbird. Other characters were played by Herschel Martin, Richard Dixon and Norm Fraser (Baron von Sloucho). One character was even named Poor Slob.

Of these characters, Thompson quotes Bramming as saying: "Corky would dress up like a mummy whenever we showed a mummy movie. We did crazy things and the show had no time limit. Sometimes our breaks in the movie lasted ten minutes!" Back then all the skits were live, and viewers could often hear a stagehand's muffled laughter in the background. Bramming later said: "The movies weren't really scary, and there was never any blood and gore in the movies or in our segments…we were there to have fun."

He wasn't kidding about the movies. "Donovan's Brain" with Nancy Davis (later Reagan) was about a brain kept alive in a tank. Not bad, actually. It aired on Oct. 27, 1961. However, other movies were just plain awful, so much so that they were laughable. One in particular, "Missile to the Moon," used the same soundtrack for the screams that was in another classic,

Sir Cecil Creape, portrayed by Russ McGown, hosts another episode of WSM-TV show "Creature Feature." (Jeff Thompson)

"Attack of the 50 Foot Woman." The scenery did not match in the background and the huge, fake spider had clearly visible wires controlling it. The monsters—huge walking rocks—moved slowly, and the acting itself was pitiful. It was so bad it was good. We had a blast watching that one.

The type of movies shown and the guest characters varied. On Oct. 16, 1959, "Monster from Mars" was shown, and the Banner's "Watching Machine" column by Red O'Donnell stated that "Host (Shocko) Ken Bramming introduces 3 live weirdies: Frantic Freddy, Wolf Boy and Vampira." On Oct. 23, "Shock Theater" ran the classic "Monster Maker," and on Oct. 30, 1959, one day before Halloween, the Nashville Banner reported that "Ken Bramming hosts a Spook Party at 10:15." The featured presentation that night was "Panther's Claw." On Oct. 7, 1960, the TV listing was called "The Mystic Circle" with emcee Dr. Lucifur. The Lon Chaney epic, "Calling Dr. Death," was the attraction.

On a cool October night in 1961, my friend Sam and I watched "The Ape" with Boris Karloff. It was not really that scary but believable enough to make us boys wonder if the ape could be lurking about in trees or in the bushes within the neighborhood. Unfortunately for Sam, as soon as Dr. Lucifur ended the show at midnight in his Transylvanian accent, saying, "Good night and pleasant dreams!," it was time for him to go home. Sam lived across my backyard, through some hedges and at the other end of Herbert's Field, which at that hour of night in the autumn was quite dark. I remember telling him to watch out for the ape. As he stepped out through the back door and into the darkness, I let out a scream. I could hear him spouting obscenities as he scampered at full speed through the hedge row and out of sight. I later on received an extra helping of vulgarities from Sam, who was none too pleased with my send-off.

During the early 1960s, "Shock Theater" was so popular the show was re-aired again on Sunday afternoons around the lunch hour. It was called "Shock Jr.," and I often ate on a TV tray and took in a horror classic, usually right after getting home from church, much to the chagrin of my mother.

Times began to change, and by 1967 "Shock Theater" left WSIX. It returned briefly between October 1968 and November 1969, with Dr. Lucifur once again at the helm of a weekend horror movie on the independent station WMCV-TV 17. Channel 17 even threw a Halloween party for kids in October 1968 in which Bramming appeared as Dr. Lucifur, and his sidekick Corky Savely showed up as the mummy.

By 1970 Dr. Lucifur and "Shock Theater" were no longer found on the airwaves. However, a new Saturday-night horror telecast on WSM-TV Channel 4 came on the scene in the early '70s. It was called "Creature Feature," and the host was a new TV horror character, Sir Cecil Creape (Russ McCown). As if a resurrected Dr. Lucifur was in the studio, Ken Bramming provided the introduction in his inimitable voice. Sir Creape often mentioned his friend Dr. Lucifur and even invited him for a late-night appearance on one show.

For my friends and me, "Shock Theater" and Dr. Lucifur faded away as we moved further into our high-school years. College days came along and that entire period became a childhood memory. Aging has a way of resurrecting youth, and seeing an old horror classic from decades ago conjures up the image of a sinister-looking Transylvanian with an eye patch, cape and cigarette holder once again asking us to go with him "into the supernatural, fantasy, and the world beyond." I wish I could. "Good night and pleasant dreams!"

CHAPTER 19

Trips, Signs and Automobiles

DURING THE late 1940s and into the 1950s, America witnessed an automobile boom. We had survived two wars and a depression, and all the servicemen had for the most part returned home to their girlfriends and wives to purchase homes in the suburbs. Family units were in vogue. Rationing had ended, the rubber supply had picked up and gasoline prices were cheap, as were the prices of automobiles. Automakers took notice of this newfound optimism and freedom. Production skyrocketed, not only with cars but big cars. The 1950 DeSoto Custom had a wheelbase over 139 inches. Most were V-8s and seated six to eight comfortably. By the end of the '50s, over 40 million automobiles were on the roads. The car culture expanded Nashville and radically changed our city.

In this 1949 photo, taken by a road somewhere in Georgia, the author entertains his sisters, Lynn and Beth, and his mother during a vacation trip.

Woody Miller's Gulf station on Murphy Road in 1957. (Woody Miller Jr.)

Broadway was a buyer's smorgasbord in the early 1950s. Dealers on the street included: E. Gray Smith (Packard), W.G. Baker Motor Co.; Jim Reed (Chevy); Cumberland Motor Co. (Dodge-Plymouth); Kaiser-Frazer Motors; Hippodrome Motors (Ford); Nashville Motors (Buick); Capitol Chevrolet; Liddon Pontiac; R.L. Parnell (DeSoto-Plymouth); King Nash Motors (Nash Rambler) and Ralph Nichols. Palmer-Hooper Motors sold Lincoln-Mercury on West End Avenue.

Some others in and around downtown were: Shackleford Buick, Coggin Chevrolet, Paul Mountcastle Motors, Maxey and Donnelly (Studebaker), Beaman Motor Co., Central Motor Co., Oak Motors, Crown Motors, Comer Sales, Dressler-White Co., and Ben Polk Chevy in Goodlettsville.

New car prices were affordable to say the least. King Nash sold the 1951 Nash Rambler convertible for $1,095. In 1953, Kaiser-Frazer advertised the "Henry J" for $1,399 and offered weekly payments of $9.49. That same year Liddon Pontiac displayed a newspaper clip-out of a $100 Confederate bill you could redeem on any used car over $1,000 during their great "Dixieland Sale." The ad stated, "This offer is also good for all Yankees, converted or unconverted." That did not apply to my family.

With the rubber supply in full production tire prices were rock bottom. In 1953 All State tires cost $16.95. B.F. Goodrich sold a tire for $11.95 or you could buy used tires for only $4.95 at McDowell Tire at 15th and Broadway.

Finding a place to fill up with gas and having an attendant wipe the windshield, check the tire pressure and look under the hood was no problem either, for over 300 full-service "filling stations" provided that service in our community.

Many more things now took place in and were associated with our cars. You could easily commute to property elsewhere and go anywhere in less time and with more convenience than ever before. Downtown shopping was only minutes from the surrounding area. The drive-in movie and drive-in restaurant craze hit its peak in the 1950s, as did trips to vacation spots and Sunday afternoon drives. Visits to relatives in other cities that once seemed so far away did not seem so far away anymore. We went every Sunday to my grandparents in Franklin. A 20-mile tour of open farmland on the Hillsboro Pike between Nashville and their home on Lewisburg Pike, it was like a drive out in the country back then, a pleasure trip that usually took about 30 minutes. Others just loaded up the family in the car and cruised around the community. It was a ritual to some.

To hear my parents say we were going on a vacation to the beach made my imagination run wild. I remember seeing our Ford Country Squire "Woody" loaded up with luggage, fishing rods, blankets and pillows and watching my mother and older sisters pack coolers and fill the Thermos for on-the-road picnics. I usually went with Dad to Pat Patterson's Esso service station down the street from the Hippodrome Roller Rink on West End to get the car checked out for the long journey. That was the manly thing to do.

The author and his family load up the Ford Woody for a Sunday trip to visit relatives in Franklin.

One of the numerous concrete, roadside picnic tables the author's family used for lunch during road trips, this one in 1953.

Roads back then were just that, roads. The Eisenhower Interstate system was not designated until 1956, with only 1.8 miles of I-65 opening at the Alabama/Tennessee state line in 1958. So we traveled the two-lane paths for almost 20 years. U.S. highway signs had that familiar six-pointed oval design and were the ones in the best shape. The state signs varied in looks from state to state. Many were triangular in appearance. Local routes usually had a circle around the number. When we drove on those our shock absorbers were tested to the max. There was nothing like traveling the old highway across Monteagle Mountain. Our state was known as the "detour state" in the 1920s due primarily to the inability to traverse that land mass. Finally, a road was built across it in 1923 and remained until 1962 when I-24 was constructed. Those hairpin curves going up and coming down are still fresh in my mind.

The highways on our vacation drives to Florida, Fort Morgan, Ala., or to the southwest took us through most every small town. There were no detours around the business district. Each community looked as if business was booming. Traffic was everywhere, horns honked, and folks crossed the street just in front of you. Most waved as you went by, recognizing the out-of-state license tag.

Gas stations were prevalent, mainly Gulf, Esso, Sinclair, Pure, Mobilgas and Texaco. We usually stopped there to fill up, use the rest room and to buy a soft drink. I recall those red-and-white "Drink Coca-Cola in Bottles" machines with six selections enclosed in glass in a long column. Cost in the early '50s was displayed in bold lettering: 10 cents. Drink machines at those stations often contained Brownie Chocolate drink, Cream Soda, Nehi, Fanta, Frostie Root Beer as well as the "friendly pepper upper."

Sign poles at cross streets usually had six or seven towns shown with arrows pointing which way to go. I became pretty good at deciphering which road to take for my dad (most of the time).

Back out on the open road, around lunch time, we would just pull over to the side of the road where there was often a large, concrete picnic table expressly for travelers. They were huge, as seating could accommodate eight hungry vacationers. My mother and sisters would unpack the homemade sandwiches, pull out the Thermos (the type that had those round, concealed cups under the lid) and spread a tablecloth over the top. Large, 50-gallon trash barrels sat nearby for any leftover debris. Litter was rarely seen around those spots. Most every town had these iconic eating areas out in the rural countryside. It was something we looked forward to. On the occasions when those cement dining structures were not in the area, we would spread a large sheet out on the ground and eat right there in an open area located off of the road a bit. Safety was no real issue back in those days.

After eating we boarded our non-air conditioned vehicle and continued back on the two-lane. The first mass-marketed air conditioner for cars with dash controls was in 1954, made specifically for the Nash models. Pontiac also had them in 1954 but by 1960 only 20 percent of all cars in the U.S. had air-conditioning. We kept cool on all of our trips in the 1950s by employing the hand-crank method. The summer heat circulating through the open windows, the constant bumping of the road, sounds of the wind and nearby passing vehicles all combined to create a slumbering environment. I could feel that warm, drugged feeling and the heavy pull on my eyes begin to take place. It eventually put a young kid like me to sleep. I usually woke up with a slight drool and a sweaty pillow.

If we drove at night I often sat up front with my dad and tried to find a baseball game on the AM radio. We usually picked up a faraway station and could hear the announcer intermittently between the fade outs and static as he broadcast the game. It was kind of magical to hear a game of nines being played and us in the dark in the middle of rural America.

To pass the hours spent on rural highways we played road games. One was counting cows, but only on your side of the car. Back then cows were plentiful and easy to spot on rolling hillsides. The first one to 100 was the winner, and it usually would take less than an hour depending on what state we were in. Should someone spot a graveyard, all the cow points you had were wiped out. Family graves were prevalent in those days and often were seen adjoining homesteads.

The alphabet game was another; any sign, billboard, etc., was fair game starting with the letter "a" and progressing all the way through the alphabet. The first one to "z" was the victor, but the game usually ended when we hit "q" for long periods of time. The license plate game was similar, with the object being to spot all of the states that appeared in alphabetical order. It was rare to finish that one also.

Road signs, billboards and shoulder markers provided some level of familiarity, especially when a long way from home. The "See Rock City" promos on barns and ones that proclaimed you could "See 7 States" were always a welcome sight and were in most every state we used to drive through.

By far my favorite road signs were the Burma-Shave advertisements. Those six little, red-and-white wooden signs, each several hundred yards apart, kept you watching for the punch line that always ended with "Burma-Shave." It was an idea conjured up by Allan Odell to promote a brushless shaving cream to his father Clinton. It took off in 1925 and lasted until 1963. It cheered up folks during the Great Depression and World War II and humored us during the '50s. At one point over 7,000 graced our highways. Some of my favorites went like this:

The wolf
Is shaved
So neat and trim
Red Riding Hood
Is chasing him
Burma-Shave

Soap
May do
For lads with fuzz
But sir, you ain't
What you wuz
Burma-Shave

The hero
Was brave and strong
And willin'
She felt his chin
Then wed the villain
Burma-Shave

Some even offered warnings:

The one who
Drives when
He's been drinkin'
Depends on you
To do his thinkin'
Burma-Shave

By the late 1960s interstates and wide, four-lane roads were constructed to accommodate the demand for more efficient travel, faster cars and to connect big cities with one another. The old roads I took on family trips and long vacations were now bypassed by freeways. Gazing out of our windows on rural roads and counting cows or spotting family graveyards to erase my sister's point totals became rare. The small-town restaurants, service stations and markets that sat on highways directly on our route were now off the beaten path. Many dried up and vanished as part of progress. It was a slower pace back then, with a down-home feel. We cannot physically journey to the past, only mentally, but that is good enough, I suppose. But for me:

> *I wish*
> *I could*
> *Drive back in time*
> *And see again*
> *Those signs that rhyme*
> *Burma-Shave*

CHAPTER 20

The Local Drug Store

IN 1925 the General Drug Store opened downtown at 802 Church Street on the corner of 8th Avenue North. It featured an expansive counter serving food, soda and ice cream, as well as a cigar center, all run by Dallas Neil. At that same time (and until the mid-1940s) the Vanderbilt Pharmacy, operated by the popular Doc Taylor, was the place to go for Vandy students. His sons continued the tradition into the '50s when they became Commodores themselves.

By the time the 1950s and '60s rolled around there were close to 100

This photo from a private collection appeared in the March 7, 1990, Nashville Banner captioned: "Soda jerks, at right, and customers pose for what could be a grand opening of General Drug Store at 802 Church St., 1925."

of these drug store/pharmacies in operation, many with those familiar orange-and-blue Rexall signs adorning the front. There was Acklen Park and Waldrum's. Battlefield Pharmacy, Warner Drugs and J.P. Brown were on Franklin Road. Mincy's, Elliston Place Soda Shop, Yates Pharmacy, Green Hills Pharmacy, Bradshaw Drugs, Blankenship and Gus Drugs were popular. There was also: Henry Drugs (West End), Madison Drugs, Peach Pharmacy (downtown on 4th), Johnson Drugs (Hillsboro Road), Garrett Drug, Winters Pharmacy (Buchanan), Haddox and Stevens (Charlotte), and Belle Meade Drugs (Harding Road). The then up-and-coming chains Wilson-Quick and Walgreens in Green Hills Village had a presence as well. Most all of these were locally owned and operated by the pharmacists living nearby.

Right after Labor Day of 1941, at 4006 Granny White Pike, Curtis Hutcherson set up shop across from David Lipscomb College. Next-door businesses included a barber shop, Landon Hardware, a cleaners and A&S Market, where Hutcherson would buy food out of good will even though it cost more than in his pharmacy. It was a great location, particularly after he became a resident on nearby Graybar Lane.

At age 14 Jack Bradshaw began work for "Hutch" doing deliveries. When Pearl Harbor was attacked, Bradshaw (who later opened Bradshaw Drugs) was sent out on the delivery bike to notify area patrons of the disaster. He would also deliver prescriptions, Cokes and cigarettes on his two-wheeler. At that time the store was "out in the country," and delivery on a bike at night could be cold and frightening. No matter, though—the customers had to get their items, particularly the elderly. Hutcherson also offered curb service provided by the soda jerks who took out Cokes and sandwiches to waiting motorists.

The canopied store featured a long soda fountain, cash register, cigar case, and later a peanut machine at the front. Round stools with red tops and black beads bordered the fountain where all the food and real ice-cream shakes were prepared. At the back of the store there were a couple of booths where Pat Boone, girlfriend Shirley, and many Lipscomb kids often met after school. Past those booths was the pharmacy section, slightly elevated, where Hutcherson and his assistants filled prescriptions. Over the years his assistants included Paul Carmen, Bill Staggs, Randall Simmons and Ed Daniel. Dottie

A customer enters Hutcherson's Pharmacy circa 1972. Opened in 1941, Hutcherson's was located across from David Lipscomb College for over four decades until it closed.

Chastain kept the books, and a black lady named Christine was hired to help with the fountain area and cash register. Hutherson was one of the first to hire a black person. She was described as a "wonderful, friendly woman."

Across from the soda fountain was the store area where gift items, perfume and over-the-counter medicinal supplies were displayed. There were also the penny candy, magazine rack and some comic books toward the front. It was not a big place but one that many called home for four decades. In later years, the old timers, or Liars Club, consisting of former employees and patrons, met there for coffee.

Daughter Mary Eve (Hutherson) Lingbloom worked briefly at the pharmacy but admits she found it challenging to make change from the cash register. A big deal, I suspect, where the profit margin is concerned. She practically lived at the store, sitting on a stool by the prescription counter hours on end, learning life lessons from her father on how to treat people.

The other daughter, Patricia, recalls that the highlight of her day in the early 1960s was getting off from school and scurrying to the store for a habit-forming cherry Coke. It was a ritual. She said it was not unusual for their

Pharmacist Curtis "Doc" Hutcherson (in white coat) converses with customers at his soda fountain circa 1972. Such fountains were common in drug stores and served everything from ice cream to grilled sandwiches.

father to go into the store at 2 a.m. to fill an order for someone in desperate need. This was commonplace and, by the way, his phone number was in the book.

The soda fountain was primarily manned by young neighborhood kids. One of those was Hal Rosson, whose mother was a friend of the Hutchersons. She took him down there one day in 1962, and he was hired on the spot for 60 cents an hour as a soda jerk. He worked there through high school and into his college days. Later on his brother Ron would follow in his footsteps.

Working with others such as the Tucker brothers, Les White, and the pleasant Drusilla, made for a great work environment. Rosson said he cooked 30-cent burgers greased on the flat grill with butter. He also made tuna, pimento-cheese and grilled-cheese sandwiches and served up glasses of Bromo Seltzer for those who needed it after a long night. It sounds frightening to me.

"We had this really cool barrel of root beer," Rosson recalled. It sat on the edge of the counter. Only frosted mugs were used for that beverage, which cost a whopping 5 cents. "It was like a law. Nothing could go into those mugs but root beer."

There was one patron who stretched the law, though. Once a week this man asked for a mixture of Coke, Sprite, cherry syrup, chocolate syrup, simple syrup (sugar water and lemon juice) and root beer, all in a frosted mug.

"We called the drink a 'Suicide,'" said Rosson. My guess is the gentleman floated out of the shop after a couple of swigs.

Tips were adequate, but one lady, who with her children customarily made shambles of the back booth, was put in her place by an out-of-character statement uttered by young Rosson. Working while wearing an apron, madras shirt, white Levi jeans and penny loafers with no socks, he heard the woman say as he walked away with the dirty dishes: "Evidently Doc doesn't pay his employees enough to afford socks."

Stopping in his tracks, Rosson replied: "Mrs. _____ , I buy socks with the tips I get." So there.

Deliveries in later years were done using cars, primarily Doc Hutcherson's blue station wagon with a column shift. Youngsters with no shifting experience had to learn as they drove. Getting the order to the customer quickly was foremost in Doc's philosophy. Rosson recalls stripping many a gear en route to a neighborhood home. Most of these transactions and many in the store were done on a charge basis. Bills were sent out regularly and all were expected to pay in a timely manner. When the occasional tardiness occurred, a simple "Help" in red marker was written at the bottom of the statement. This usually did the trick.

Doc Hutcherson ended his service after 45 years as the big chains undercut him and the new-found mobility of kids became prevalent. He once said he could buy from Walgreens cheaper than he could buy from his drug wholesaler. A good man left the business.

Rosson becomes choked up when he recalls that Doc told him that he could take whatever supplies he needed to go back to school—free of charge. He believes he did this for many an employee. He was always good to kids. Once two boys were scuffling and shattered a store window. The kids were not charged nor were their parents notified of the bad behavior. A lifelong friendship was established.

"He was a great guy, a legend in the community," said longtime friend Charlie Baker.

Moon Drug Co. in the Belle Meade Theater Building in 1955.

Some three miles west, in the Belle Meade Theater Building, veteran Clyde Moon opened up Moon Drug Co., branching off from Moon-McGrath Drugs at 6th and Union.

I spent the better part of my misspent youth at Moon Drug. Living only one mile away it was an easy bike ride or leisurely walk. On one side was Cooper and Martin grocery store and Gracie's, and on the other side was the Belle Meade Theater. When the grocery store closed down, Moon moved into the location, giving us back-door access in addition to a main entrance.

The theater, run by E.J. Jordon, provided Moon with a ready-made clientele, and he encouraged all patrons, especially kids, to visit Moon Drug. It was not difficult for him to do. Katherine "Kitty" Sue (Emery) Moon, Doc's daughter, reflected: "He had an eye out for my mom." Hazel Moon worked there and loved to sell candy and take road trips to purchase items for the gift section. She also kept her children Kitty and Peter in line and ran the house, as husband Clyde was a workaholic. Hazel was the backbone of the family.

Jordon's Happiness Club at Belle Meade Theater (see Chapter 25) catered to young kids, me being one. Regularly when the show ended we all flocked next door to the drug store. The long soda fountain with those swivel stools, large booths, and checkerboard floor were iconic.

Of the stools Paul Clements said, "I spun around so much one day the top came off and down I went."

Local youngster, and later a pharmacist there, Billy Meador said: "I used to blow wrappers off straws at the soda fountain and watch them fly up to the ceiling." I did that as well, much to the chagrin of Betty Lou, who worked the fountain.

Like Hutcherson's there were cherry Cokes, sodas, malts and shakes (the kind made in those large, metal cups that always had a little extra milkshake for you if you finished your glass), and hand-dipped cones made from Velvet Ice Cream.

Mainstays Shirley and the unmistakable Betty Lou (with her peroxided hair) prepared grilled delights. Stock boy George Tomlin, valued employee Gwinn, and longtime assistant pharmacist Floyd "Colonel" Martin helped make the store a lifelong memory. Joe Hendrix and Cathy Hamilton said the lady working in cosmetics was heavily made up with "huge, painted eyelashes."

Moon's had everything. Kids like me were allowed to read comics without having to buy one. A good strategy that enabled the parents to browse

This circa 1962 aerial photo shows the Belle Meade Theater Buidling and the Gracie's building. Moon Drug was located next to the theater.

about unfettered. Moon further encouraged the behavior by placing a carpet in front of the comic book stand for us to sit and read. Now that was first class. There were none of the gory kind of comics, only those that had the familiar "Approved by the Comics Code Authority" stamp. Alex Slabosky said, "I'm sure Doc Moon did not want to offend area parents." Kitty affirmed that notion: "My father created a culture of family."

There was a post office in the back, a film-developing service and even a small library where one could check out a book. Alex's mom, Molly, took full advantage of this feature. There was a phone booth inside especially for kids to call home after the movies, and a "tube-tester" center where you could buy and replace your television tubes. One had to have TV in those days; a blown tube was not a good thing.

I bought lots of cinnamon oil for soaking toothpicks and kites to fly in Herbert's Field. I also bought hundreds of Topps baseball cards with those flat, powdery pieces of bubble gum wrapped inside that left the cards smelling sweet. There were jawbreakers, bubble-gum fireballs and cigars, plus candy cigarettes and all the other standard tooth-decaying items much in demand in those days.

"Wow," said Joe Henrick who, along with his sister Betty, lived around

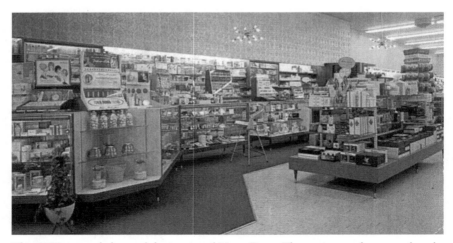

This 1976 postcard shows of the interior of Moon Drug. The caption on the postcard reads: "Nashville's largest and most modern drug store. 7 major departments. Complete prescription and sick room supplies—Cosmetics, Personalizing, Luncheonette, Sundries and Household Needs, and a U.S. Post Office." (Ridley Wills)

Original caption from the March 5, 1975, Nashville Banner: "Robert Street, left, accepts from Clyde Moon, founder of Moon Drug Store on Harding Road, the one millionth prescription to be filled by the firm since it opened in 1939. A spokesman for the Tennessee Pharmaceutical Association said available records indicate only a very few drug stores in the state have attained the one million milestone." (Nashville Public Library, Nashville Room, photo by Bob Ray)

the corner on Kenner. "Moon Drug was the center of the universe for my neighborhood." It was that for all Woodmont School kids and their families.

As Kitty got into her teens she and Margaret Shaver (Verbel) were filmed in a Moon TV advertisement that took hours to make and got her interested in a filming career.

"During the holidays we would help out wrapping Christmas presents for customers," Kitty recalled. "Just after Santa Claus would come (on Christmas Day) someone would call for a delivery." Her dad of course would go to the store to oblige. It was also not uncommon for Dr. Tom Frist's wife, Louise, to call in a prescription for a patient when her husband was not available. Doc Moon knew the family and would fill the order, no questions asked. Living in the area, customers were not only customers but friends as well.

Doc Moon was a compassionate soul. "One time my mom caught a delivery boy red-handed confiscating cigarettes and insisted that he be fired," Kitty said. "Dad told Mom that if the boy was in that bad of shape he must

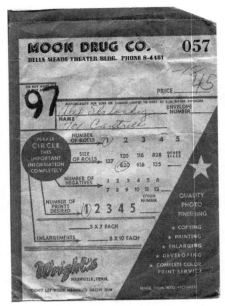

This Moon Drug photo-order envelope is from circa 1955—notice the five-digit phone number at the top. (Alex Slabosky)

have trouble feeding his family as well." The boy remained a long-time employee.

"[Dad] wouldn't so much as take a dime that wasn't his. He loved people," said Kitty.

Doc Moon's smiling face behind the pharmacy counter and his benevolence were part of his persona and why Moon's was such a success. Both Hazel and Clyde were "wonderful, wonderful people," said Meador.

As with most of these owner-operated neighborhood shops, items not paid for in cash were just written down on paper and later billed. Many a time I would get water balloons, candy, ball cards, or eat at the soda fountain and get up and say, "Just charge it to my parents." No questions were asked…except when my folks would get the statement. I was often told to tone down my very important purchases.

Just like Hutcherson's, Clyde Moon's store also faded away, a victim of the almighty dollar and a changing culture. He filled prescriptions and greeted customers all the way up to age 90. He was the face that drove the business. Moon's, Hutcherson's, and others like them, eventually disappeared, and with them went a major piece of Americana, leaving a void in the fabric of our neighborhoods. Back in those days neighborhoods were king, and the local drug store served as the focal point.

Speaking about Hutcherson, Mary Eve stated of her father, "His role model for public service was why I became a public services worker myself. We hardly ever had a holiday meal when daddy did not leave us to fill a prescription for a sick child. That was his work ethic—to help people. … I was so proud of my father and the kind of man he was."

Of her dad Kitty recalls a dinner discussion with relatives when she was

6 concerning cheating in school, with specific examples being given by the adults. Her father was asked point-blank if he had cheated, and the room went quiet. His modest answer of "never, ever did" prompted a relative to respond: "Clyde, I wish I could say the same." Honesty and integrity were his lifelong trademarks.

"Quite an example for me and Peter," Kitty said.

Those men were part of that small microcosm in time when handshakes and spoken words were your bond. I for one am grateful to have known men like that and most fortunate to still have etched in my memory what those wonderful days were like.

CHAPTER 21

1966

That's life
That's what all the people say
You're riding high in April,
Shot down in May
But I know I'm gonna change that tune
When I'm back on top, back on top in June
—Frank Sinatra, "That's Life" (1966)

THAT PRETTY much mirrored the start of 1966 for me. I was having a blast in Florida, playing ball and hanging out on the beach without a care. Failure to attend college classes was of no concern...just yet. March arrived and I had to come back home for the funeral of my wonderful grand-dad, a solemn occasion. Going back to school, I was hit by a loss of a scholar-ship funds and a non-renewal of my college status as a student. Begging to an unsympathetic art history teacher for an upgrade proved fruitless. My inevi-table military re-classification landed on deaf ears to Dr. Schidler. I returned home at the end of May to my "comfort zone."

Our society seemed to be changing during that year. Race riots in Watts the previous year and those led by Stokely Carmichael throughout the U.S. left everyone uneasy. Draft-card burnings, B-52 bombings of North Vietnam and anti-war demonstrations picked up. The cancer scare from smoking became a reality when the requirement of a label stating "Caution, Cigarette Smoking May Be Hazardous To Your Health" became common on all cig-arette packs. John Lennon's remark—"We are more popular than Jesus"—raised eyebrows, and a man named Richard Speck murdered eight nurses in

Chicago. A more per-
missive America seemed
to be on the horizon.
The go-go scene was fir-
ing up with gyrating girls
in tight tops, mini-skirts
and boots. That part I
could deal with.

On the tube at
WLAC Channel 5 was
"Secret Agent Man,"
with Johnny Rivers
singing the theme.
"Hullabaloo" was in its
last season. Dick Clark's
"Where the Action Is"
featuring hosts Paul
Revere and the Raiders,
among others, and
Freddy Cannon singing
the original theme, was

In June 1966, the author and his father took a float trip down the White River. Here they are pictured on the banks of the river frying freshly-caught trout.

a hit. It aired on ABC Channel 2. "I Dream of Jeannie" with the luscious
Barbara Eden corralled all the males to Channel 4.

"Who's Afraid of Virginia Woolf" was at a theater downtown, accompanied by a warning for the under-18 crowd, as was "The Good, the Bad and
the Ugly." My favorite, "Dracula, Prince of Darkness" with Christopher Lee,
frightened all the gals, and "Batman, The Movie" came out.

With no plans really, I played the young kid role. I slept late, shot baskets
in my backyard, went out with my friends who were home from college for
the summer, and enjoyed late-night beverages and pizza in the Keg Room at
the House of Pizza on White Bridge Road.

My dad finally determined it was time for some father-and-son quality time away from Nashville. We went to the hills of Arkansas and spent
several days getting blistered and catching trout during a float trip on the

rural White River, directed by Miller's Float Service just outside the tiny town of Cotter on Trout Dock Trail. Camping out at night, rinsing off in the river and grilling freshly-caught trout was both fun and a bit inconvenient. Bathing in the cold water was a shriveling experience, and the campout in a tent on the river bank led to a couple of sleepless evenings, exacerbated by our guide's warning about wild boar roaming the area at night. It was a good time for both of us.

In July I went to see the Young Rascals, Shades of Blue, the Knickerbockers, B.J. Thomas and others in concert at the Municipal Auditorium. The show almost ended in bedlam when one of the Rascals broke a guitar string and threw it into the crowd. The inane teens fought over it, creating cuts galore.

During that time Skateland on Gallatin Road showcased local bands such as the Charades and the Kapers. Cooper and Martin grocery stores presented "Let's Go to the Races" on Channel 5 on Saturday nights and Figure 8 races were held at the Fairgrounds.

I went to many combos, finding myself being entertained once in the

Original caption from the July 9, 1966, Nashville Banner: "Part of a crowd of several hundred Nashville and Davidson County young men and women enjoy music of The Shifters combo during the rally as they respond to Buford Ellington's campaign for governor." The author attended this event, which took place in Belle Meade Plaza. (Nashville Public Library, Nashville Room, photo by Jack Gunter)

Thayer General Hospital, opened by the U.S. Army in 1943, was located on White Bridge Road at the site of today's Nashville State Community College. Operating as the veterans hospital in its final years, it was razed in the 1960s.

Belle Meade Plaza parking lot by the Shifters, who had an open-air party for gubernatorial hopeful Buford Ellington. Underage drinking was prevalent. I was aghast but blended in well.

> *Hot town, summer in the city*
> *Back of my neck getting dirty and gritty*
> *Been down, isn't it a pity*
> *Doesn't seem to be a shadow in the city*
> *All around, people looking half dead*
> *Walking on the sidewalk, hotter than a match head*
> —The Lovin Spoonful, "Summer in the City" (1966)

That tune was a fitting one for the rest of the summer. With pressure to do something constructive and needing capital to waste on my evening adventures, I looked for a summer job. A couple of high-school friends found a place where wages were $2.25 an hour. That was way above minimum wage. Problem was they quit after two days because the labor was too tough. The job was to demolish the old Veterans Administration Hospital buildings, also known as Thayer General, on White Bridge Road, to prepare for the construction of Nashville State Community College. Thayer housed POWs as well as returning soldiers and vets from WWII and Korea. The job entailed the

The author in July 1966 after arriving home from a summer job demolishing the old Thayer army hospital.

manual salvaging of usable lumber from the concrete and wooden buildings and the destroying of the remnants. We were to scale to the roof-tops and, with picks in hand, pry off the two-by-fours and stack them on the ground. Hailey Destruction Company was in charge of the demoli-tion. I was determined to last, particularly after my buddies, George, Billy and John, had given up after two days. It was stifling. No telling what temperature it was on those roofs. A Nashville Banner headline of July 13, 1966, stated, "Heat Wave to stay at Least 5 Days." The temperature that day was 100.

Ricky Chambers, Allen Patton and myself, all aging teens, braved the elements. We initially started at 8 a.m. and quit at 3 p.m., but the oppressive heat caused our employer to push back the hours. We subsequently began at 5 a.m. and left at noon. There were three black men who were regulars and who seemed undaunted by the heat. I only remember one of their names—Tiny. He was a large albino with a gravely voice and a head scarf, and whose famous line "Go on home to momma" was frequently directed at us, par-ticularly when we would come down for water and complain. We were told never to get caught drinking water and taking a break. That was grounds for dismissal. Always on the lookout for boss man, we could usually spot him by seeing the distant dust trails kicked up by his two-door sedan—seen from our vantage point atop a crumbling unit—as he made his way over the sprawl-ing complex. Poor Rick wanted to quit in the worst way, but hearing "Go on home to momma" made him hang on. He had a heat stroke after day one and was out a few days. I had to be taken to our pediatrician, Dr. Overall, by my mother for fluid depletion. I had an epic headache.

A couple of weeks had passed, and Al and I were prying up boards from the flooring of one of the cabins near the front, when all of a sudden he lets out an "Owww!" With a painful expression he raised one foot in the air and fell backwards. That was followed by a contorted, even more pained grimace and a mumbled string of expletives. I went over to help him up and asked "What the hell happened?"

Al, barely audible, said, "I stepped on a nail...and sat on two more."

Allen's day ended and the tetanus shots began. Regardless, Allen, Rick and I returned determined to stick it out. Heat stroke, heat exhaustion and a punctured rear end aside, no "Go on home to momma" for us.

We did watch many new workers come and go. One father-and-son team was especially memorable. The regulars called the eldest "Nub." I thought it was a belittling term, for the poor man had only one arm. Thankfully he took no exception because he had just been released from Central State Mental Hospital. He later persuaded his son, affectionately known as "Nub Jr.," to try his hand at the pick. During this sweltering period, Junior climbed up on one of the old units and began to work away. After about an hour he had disappeared. "Where is Nub Jr.?" was the word. Looking out over the dusty, mirage-like waves of heat and ruins of buildings, we spotted him moving at a fast clip down White Bridge Road. Seems he was an experienced "wine taster" and, mixed with the elements, an adverse reaction had occurred. According to Nub Sr., Junior had that reaction to all work. Nub Sr. failed to make the end of the week as well.

We three white kids eventually earned the respect of the three black men. They asked us to come to "their place" for beer and pizza on the weekends. With the riots in Watts barely over and the tension high among races in Nashville as well, we nonetheless decided to go. Might not have been smart, but away we went to a small shack down a short driveway off of Jefferson Street where the name "Shirley and Marie's" was painted across the top. After a minute or two of apprehension we went in. Dark linoleum floors with maybe six or seven tables surrounded by hard-back wooden chairs were in the center. An old jukebox full of 45-rpm records was off to the side. A large hole in the wall fronted by a counter was all we could see.

Tiny and his friends met us. They gave us pitchers of beer, pizza and dropped a quarter in the jukebox, which seemed to only play "Hold on I'm Coming" by Sam and Dave. We always left before it got too late, as the cliental became less accepting of our presence. As long as Tiny and friends hung around we were okay. It

The author and his father are pictured at Fort Campbell, Ky., in October 1966 at the author's graduation from basic training. Notice the similarity of the barracks to those in the Thayer Hospital picture on page 163.

was, as they say, "good times." Amazing how folks can get along when not influenced by large groups.

"I often think about that job," said Allen. "We stepped up and handled a nasty and tough job and proved something to ourselves in doing this. We got an experience that few have."

And on top of that we made $2.25 an hour.

By the time August arrived I received a letter. A chilling "Greetings" notice indicating I was being drafted into the U.S. Army. Not an ideal time to get such news. Demonstrations against the Vietnam War were spreading, and images from Southeast Asia were broadcast nightly on television while news anchor Walter Cronkite painted a dour picture.

Not wanting to be a foot soldier or a draft dodger but feeling like I should serve my country regardless, I enlisted in the "Buddy System"(turned out to be a misnomer). I took my physical inspection downtown with a host of other wide-eyed teens clad only in our Fruit-of-the-Looms. After being told my blood pressure was too high I decided to wait a few minutes and try again. I felt bad for my "buddy" Mallernee because he passed. After another reading I was cleared and prepared to go. My enlistment date was set for August 22.

That month was kind of a blur but the world did not stop because I was slated to go into the service. Our city announced new pay phones would be replacing the old ones. These would have just one opening for all coins; evidently it was confusing patrons to put coins into each slot. The Exotics teamed with the Spiedels to entertain sororities and frat boys all over town; Len Rossi and Mario Milano scuffled with the Mysterious Medics Saturday Aug. 20 on "All Star Wrestling" that aired on Channel 8; "Dr. Zhivago" played at the Green Hills Theater; "Shock Theater" continued to show "classics" at 10:30 p.m.; and John R, Hoss Allen, Gene Nobles and Herman Grizzard kept me tuned in to WLAC 1510 radio for those rarely-heard blues tunes and baby chick specials.

On Aug. 21, "Holiday on Ice" brought its skate extravaganza to the Municipal Auditorium with prices from $1.90 to $4. I was a no-show there. On Aug. 22, as I was heading to Clarksville for enlistment with a bus load of other poor souls, "Hanky Panky" by Tommy James and the Shondells (one of my least favorite songs) echoed down the aisles on a small radio, and the Nashville Banner headline read, "B-52s Again Hit Two Bases"—the article reported that a terrorist had injured four servicemen and a civilian by tossing a grenade at a military jeep in Saigon. Boy, was I excited.

The army barracks I called home for the next two months were eerily similar to ones I had torn down just a few weeks earlier in Nashville. Camping out on the White River banks was not comparable to the "sleep overs" we had somewhere on the fort. It was hot during basic training. Kids got heat stroke, invoking memories of the times spent on those blistering roofs of the V.A., but now there was no Nub, Nub Jr., Tiny or friends Al and Rick. They had all gone on their separate ways. There was no going home to momma either.

I survived basic training and paraded through graduation ceremonies in October. My parents and friend Dave came up for the event. My next orders were for Fort Leonard Wood in Missouri, known affectionately as Fort Lost in the Woods. Indeed it was. After another six to eight weeks of "advanced" training, and missing Thanksgiving, my father came to get me for Christmas. We even gave another soldier a ride to his home town in Gainsboro so he could be home as well. It was none too soon.

Original headline and caption from the Dec. 24, 1966, Nashville Banner: "Nature Adds To Beauty—Nature added her own decoration to the glittering Christmas tree in Memorial Square when she dumped a heavy snow providing Nashville and the state with a white Christmas." (Nashville Public Library, Nashville Room, photo by Bob Ray)

Nashville was bustling for the holidays. Decorations were everywhere and the first showing of "How the Grinch Stole Christmas" frightened and elated all the kiddos on Channel 5. "Petticoat Junction" and "Family Affair" both made their initial appearances, and the new party game Twister was a top gift for the season. For the particular gourmet, Morrison's Cafeteria at 1720 West End Ave. served up a sensational deal of old-fashioned chicken stew and dumplings for the bargain price of 39 cents. That had to be prime stuff. I spent a few hours clutching porcelain after downing a poorly-cooked baked potato with cheese, and I never returned.

Seeing old friends, sleeping late and visiting with family was a welcomed departure from military life. It was memorable for a snowstorm that hit on the 23, leaving us with 5 inches on the ground and temperatures dropping from 16 to 8 degrees, assuring all of us of the third white Christmas in 95 years. What a Christmas it was.

The year 1966 was up and down for me, kind of like the Skyliner at Fair Park. I learned a lot from my experiences but did not realize it until later in life. It was a character-building year for me, but I will leave that to my peers to decide. If given a choice, I would have skipped it altogether.

CHAPTER 22

Combo Crazy

BILL HALEY and His Comets' "Crazy Man, Crazy" hit No. 12 on the Billboard Juke Box chart June 20, 1953, and was the first rock 'n' roll recording to be played on national television. Six kids with guitars, a sax, drums and lead singer were believed to be the beginning of the "combo" craze that swept our city from the mid-1950s to the mid-1960s. Rock 'n' roll disc jockey Alan Freed and movies such as "Rock Around the Clock" and "Don't Knock the Rock" brought those boys and others to prominence just as the Baby Boomers began moving toward their teenage years. These small bands, or combos, provided the fuel for this emerging generation. I saw it all happen.

The Gators Combo, lead by Ed Hoge, was so popular that the Black Poodle in Printer's Alley held them over continually in the early 1960s. In 1957 Ed's little brother Peyton would watch them rehearse at their home on Lone Oak and would hop up and bang on the drums when the group would take a break.

Three of the Nobles in 1960 (left to right): Rusty James, Peyton Hoge and Tommy Payne. Drummer Tommy Bumpas had to leave just before this was taken. (Payton Hoge)

The Charades at the Municipal Auditorium when they opened for Herman's Hermits in 1965 (left to right): Owsley Manier, Allen Tanksley, Peyton Hoge, Jerry Smith and Jim Ragland (hidden in background). (Russel Ray Studios)

Peyton Hoge formed his own combo, called the Nobles, in 1959 with two other Belmont Methodist Church kids, Tommy Payne and Carl Crowley. He became lead singer and played a solid-black Silvertone guitar. He honed his vocal skills listening to the Sons of the Pioneers harmonize to "Tumbling Tumbleweeds" on a 78-rpm record when in the fifth grade at Burton Elementary.

The Nobles "professional" debut at the Woodmont Elementary School graduation dance was held on the patio of Dr. B.T. Bennett in 1960. They wore gold tuxedo coats with black windowpane striping and black pants. Their first song was Chuck Berry's "Maybellene."

Hoge's mother was the secretary at the school and drew up the contract paying the Nobles and her son a whopping $30 to play from 8 to 10:30 p.m. Neighbors complained about the noise, but the kids loved it and word-of-mouth set the group on its way.

Over the next few years they played on driveways at private homes, the YWCA dance for teens, sorority and frat rush parties, the Chicken Coop, high-school dances and the Cain-Sloan Teenage Fashion Show in August of 1966 (in which my wife, Carolyn, participated). They won the North High School Battle of the Bands talent show and played at the Cedars of Lebanon

State Park Hay Ride. For the latter gig, Hoge journeyed from Nashville behind an 18-wheeler on a trailer loaded with amorous teens frolicking in the hay on their way to Lebanon.

Hoge joined the Charades in 1963 as lead singer, and eventually they were recorded by local deejay Noel Ball in a studio upstairs next to Tootsie's Orchid Lounge.

In 1965 they opened for Herman's Hermits, the Shangri-Las, and Wayne Fontana and the Mindbenders in front of 10,000 screaming fans at the Municipal Auditorium. Guitarist Jerry Smith told Hoge just before they went on stage, "I think I am going to throw up." Not sure Peter Noone would have approved. I'm sure Mrs. Brown's daughter would not have.

Band mates Owsley Manier, Allen Tanksley, Jim Ragland and Drew Nixon rounded out the combo for that night. Their outfits, purchased from York's Men Store in the Arcade, were shiny, silvery sharkskin suits. Pants were really tight and the coats had narrow lapels. They finished off their look with black Beatle boots, white shirts and slim, dark ties—all influenced by the "British Invasion" of 1964. They also adopted the Dave Clark Five look, sporting white pants and blue double-breasted blazers.

The "invasion" channeled girls away from athletes and more to band members, according to Hoge. "You spotted someone cute dancing in front

The Exotics in 1967 (left to right): Glenn Crowell, Jeff Cook, Loy Hardcastle and Billy Adair.
(Glenn Crowell)

of you and all you had to do was ask who she was. Getting dates became pretty easy."

As for the audiences, "There was no violence to speak of," Hoge said. "State Trooper Buck Ross and Sgt. Edison made sure of that. They were not intimidating but friendly. [They] liked the teenagers and liked us. They were at most of our gigs."

Hoge related a high-

The Saturns Combo in 1962 (left to right): Jack Jackson, Pat Patrick and Frank Stevens. (Pat Patrick)

light from his time in the band. While playing an outdoor combo party in the Seven Hills area, he saw the lead singer of the English group The Zombies, Colin Blunstone, make his way up the paved drive toward the band. Blunstone proceeded to grab the mic and sing The Zombie's hit "Tell Her No" with Hoge, to a startled and gasping crowd.

The Charades later changed their name to Lemonade Charades to accommodate the psychedelic movement. Hoge admits buying his first pair of pinstripe bell-bottoms at Lansky Brothers in Memphis where Elvis bought his. An ego thing I'm sure.

When Elvis Presley appeared on Ed Sullivan in 1956, 10-year-old Pat Patrick said to himself, "I can do that." Elvis was one of the first rock 'n' roll acts that involved singing while playing a guitar. It was not lost on Patrick how the girls screamed.

He lived on Skyline Drive in Green Hills, just a few streets from Julia Green School. There were 44 kids on his block alone. A next-door neighbor, Ed Graham, had some drums; another kid, Jack Jackson, had a sax; and Pat found a guitar in his grandmother's attic. He formed The Saturns Combo in 1959 with his neighborhood companions. They mimicked tunes from the radio such as "Bony Moronie" and other fast-paced numbers.

Their first performances were in a basement at the home of Gene Shanks and in the den of Montgomery Bell Academy classmate Norman Carl on New Year's Eve. Crowds were estimated to number in the 30 to 40 range. Total take was $2.50.

Their first real public show was at the seventh-grade assembly at Julia Green School on Hobbs Road. The young audience went wild. Patrick said it was an eye-opening experience. They were infused with energy and amazed at the same time.

They went on to entertain between games at the Overton Junior High basketball tourney in 1961, which to this day has reaped benefits. He still remembers the Saturns playing for The Back to School Party at the Tennessee State Fair in 1961. The lights, the sounds of the roller coaster and the smell of hog dogs, combined with their rendition of Bobby Lewis's No. 1 tune "Tossin' and Turnin'," created an unforgettable memory. It was also their first "introduction to East Nashville girls."

When they rehearsed at guitarist Bill Davidson's home during Christmas of 1961, Davidson's sister Carol, a student at Vandy, liked what she heard and asked the youngsters to perform. They played at the SAE House the

Original caption from the Aug. 22, 1965, Nashville Tennessean: "Keeny Agee, Pat Patrick and Stuart Keathly, all Vanderbilt students, are forming a new group to be called the Beach Nutz. Each of the boys has played for years with various other combos." (Jimmy Phillips)

Original caption from the Aug. 22, 1965, Nashville Tennessean: "Blue-coated Charades are lost in a crowd of dancers as they provide a solid beat for the gathering. Members of the combo are Owsley Manier, rhythm guitarist; Drew Nixon, drummer; Peyton Hoge, singer; Alan Tanksley, singer; Jerry Smith, lead guitarist; and Jim Ragland, bass guitarist. This group and others like it enjoy great demand for services for parties, personal appearances." (Jimmy Phillips)

next weekend and were so popular they were booked for the next couple of months. It was a huge breakthrough. The parents had to drive and be there to chaperone because the drinking age was nowhere near 14 and the curfew was way past their bedtime. The boys could usually be seen with turquoise shirts and black peg pants.

The combo was eventually renamed The Fabulous Beach Nutz Show Band to accommodate the surf crowd in 1964. Later they became the Kracker Jax. Above the Belle Meade Shopping Center one hot weekend, they won Nashville's Battle of the Bands contest, which eventually got them a recording contract under the name Lost in Sound. That was 1966–'67. During the group's peak years there was no need for marketing as most kids could refer them to someone else in another neighborhood school, sorority or fraternity. A call from a friend in a sorority went something like this: "We got a party next week, come on over and play on Cathy Daniel's driveway."

They were playing on the college campus at Sewanee at the Phi Gamma House when locals from Tracy City crashed the party. After requesting a particular song over and over, an inebriated crasher charged the stage. As Patrick retreated, frat brothers pinned the poor soul against the brick wall, stemming the attack. It was one of the few times they had to "unplug."

The boys performed regularly at the Tiger-a-Go Go on Charlotte, the Chicken Coop just over Nine Mile Hill and Mrs. Brown's next to Loveless Café on Highway 100. "You could get home cooking in the front and get a drink and party down in the back," said Patrick. Can't get much better than that.

A Franklin native and fellow classmate of mine at BGA, Billy Adair, saw a group called the Valiants in the seventh grade in 1959 and said to himself, "I want to do that." Plus the guitar was "cool." His parents coughed up the cash for a guitar, and he taught himself to play. His first band was called the Telstars and in his words, "We were wretched."

In 1962 at age 15, their first performance was at band mate Bubbie Beasley's home, and the crowd of 20 or so seemed to be enjoying the event. Then an individual approached Adair and said, "What are you guys making tonight?" Adair said he wasn't sure. With that the reply was, "I'll double it if you leave." Undaunted, they kept on playing.

Adair later became proficient and played with the Silhouettes in 1963– '64, rocking teenagers all over Nashville on blacktops and patios at frat houses, and they were constantly seen at Harpeth Hall and MBA.

In 1964, a regular stop was at the home of Jere Carter, a BGA student on Woodmont Boulevard. One time as they set up on the back porch expecting a crowd of 100 or so, over 1,500 people made their way in. Unbelievably, no violence occurred. There

Original caption from a 1964 Nashville Tennessean: "Members of the Kappa Phi preparatory school fraternity entertained at rush parties Monday. At the combo party held at the home of Dr. and Mrs. Oscar Carter on Woodmont Boulevard are, from left, Mary Sawyer, Bobby Joyner, Ralph McCracken, Christine Hawkins, Lynn Mabry, John Farringer, president, and Jack Jackson, sax player." (J.T. Phillips)

were always two state
troopers who didn't mind
us youngsters drinking,
so long as we were not
falling-down drunk or
coming in with a beer.
"Any trouble back in
those days and they
would call your parents,"
said Adair.

Admission was
$1.50 at the front of the
driveway. "Back then
if we weren't working
three nights a week, it
was a slow week," said
Adair. They were paid
$150 that night.

Adair began the
Exotics in late 1964
with classmate Glenn

In front of a 1964 line dance at MBA are Misty Wager and Eddie Mulligan; in the background on the right are Pat Woods, Bill Geny and Pat Patrick.

Crowell. Loy Hardcastle and Jeff Cook joined in. Promotions were by word-of-mouth, posters in drug stores and signs on poles. Eventually their reputation garnered an engagement at a Daytona Beach motel in June 1965, which I attended. The gig brought The Exotics together with the Allman Joys (later the Allman Brothers Band). They were a regular in Nashville as well. When Adair saw the long-haired kids perform, it blew him away, especially since the motel operator said they were to open for The Exotics. Duane Allman, prior to the night's performance, said to Billy, "Been hearing a lot about you around town. We'll see who is the best." Adair was speechless. The Exotics did a good job, and later the two bands jammed together and became friends. "It was the first long-haired group I had seen, and they were awesome," said Adair.

The Exotics' only real promoter was former Sewanee basketball coach Lon Varnell. After opening at the War Memorial for the nationally-famous

Standells, who recorded "Dirty Water" in 1966, Varnell said that he could not represent The Exotics anymore because they were too hard to promote. He told Adair that The Standells got upset because the Exotics were too good and the crowd became uninterested after The Exotics left the stage. "We were plain, no particular outfits. We were just good," said Adair. It was a far cry from the Telstars in 1962.

The Exotics backed up the all-black soul group the Spidells all over the South. "It was pretty tough to stop in Chattanooga to get a sandwich and have them wait in the car for us to bring out their food," recalled Adair.

At the 1966 BGA homecoming dance in George I. Briggs gym, they were hired by teacher Tony Cobb (the son of David Cobb at WSM, who coined the phrase "Music City, USA") along with the Spidells, to play for the crowd. The Spidells were very animated and had a sound and routine that would rival the Temptations. After several songs one could see the headmaster starting to fume. Finally in the middle of Junior Walker's "Shotgun," he grabbed the microphone and said to the lead singer, Billy Wright: "Young man, we don't have that kind of thing going on around here." Cobb was furious and expressed his displeasure to the headmaster while Adair told the guys that maybe they should do one more number and then leave. The crowd's energy was zapped. What a homecoming.

Scores of combos sprang up in our city during their peak in the early to mid-1960s. It was part of the youth culture. What also was part of the culture was the atmosphere and the kids who danced, drank and experienced adolescence during those brief times.

The combos of the 1960s made teenagers move and shake like never before. It was not so much the bands, their names or the musicians, but the events and atmosphere they created that is unforgettable.

My roll through combo time was during its peak from 1962 to 1966. I was heavily influenced by deejay Noel Ball, and by John R. ("Way Down South in Dixie"), Hoss Allen, Gene Nobles and their late-night radio shows on WLAC. Country music was something for rural tourists. Us kids wanted soul music, rock 'n' roll, and rhythm and blues. Combos capitalized on this new, uninhibited sound.

One summer night in 1963, I saw The Fairlanes, featuring black singer

Tack Taylor, on Harding Hill Lane. I had been to a few combo parties before and had realized something different was happening. It was Paul Clements' first live event. After seeing Taylor up close mouthing the microphone and bluesing out with "Twist and Shout," Clements too saw the light. Watching cute Mickey Miller shimmying to the beat in a tight, clingy sundress may have been a factor as well. Or perhaps it was the sultry Lyn Mabry sporting her long blonde hair and rhythmic dance moves. She always attracted the notice of us young males.

The sights and sounds that energized us within did the same thing for Baby Boomer teens all over Nashville. We got it. Adolescence had arrived and so had rock 'n' roll. It was new and unique, and we were in the middle of it. Combos were more than just four or five boys playing instruments. They conveyed to us an inner feeling never felt before. And it looked cool when the lead guitarist would put his cigarette between the strings during a number. Kids regularly smoked back then; it was accepted.

On most any summer night you could hop in your car, roll down the windows and listen for a distant voice or guitar. More often than not you were successful—a combo was playing. Walking from your car down the street to an outdoor combo party was part of the experience. The anticipation excited the soul. You could hear, but not see, the band echoing throughout the neighborhood and envision what lay ahead. Vocals of the lead singer could be heard over the guitar riffs on such tunes as "Johnny B. Goode" and the familiar party sound of "Stubborn Kind of Fellow" ("Say yeah Yeah YEAH; Say YEAH Yeah yeah.") It made you want to hurry up and get there.

Once there, girls would run to girlfriends who had arrived earlier and hug as if they had not seen them for years, when in fact only hours before they were either in math class together or had just talked on the phone. Boys often would slug down a can of Schlitz, Bud or Colt 45 to get one last buzz before making their way into the crowd. Some made grand entrances doing the Twist, the Locomotion or the Jerk. As long as you weren't falling down drunk the state troopers who provided security were unconcerned. Those neighborhood parties were open to anyone who paid a dollar at the card table at the beginning of the driveway. All were welcome so long as your behavior was under control. It was a time of camaraderie, friendship and exploration—all to a new type of sound.

Combo parties, also called "combos," provided an opportunity to get really close with your date, especially when the band slowed it down with "make-out" tunes like "Sleep Walk," "Daddy's Home," "Talk to Me," "Sincerely" or "What's Your Name?" A slow dance was nothing more than a boy and a girl with their hands wrapped around each other's waist accompanied by an occasional lean to either side. You could always tell who was or wasn't going to "get some" by the way couples held each other during those numbers.

At a 1963 combo in the Hillsboro High School gym, Mary Franklin dances with an unidentified boy, possibly doing the Shimmy or the Shing-a-ling.

Immediately after the slow tune the band would lurch into something like "Shout" or "Shotgun" which would reignite the teens into various dance moves. The familiar "two hands to one side and leg up" move, as if firing a gun, could be seen throughout the crowd.

The later in the evening, the more risqué the music became. A combo standard was Chuck Berry's "My Ding-A-Ling" and "Reelin' and Rockin'" ("Well I looked at my watch, it said a quarter to ten, I said to my baby, let's do it again"). Lines were made up as the band got into the song. Other late-night regulars were "Hey Baby, Let Me Bang Your Box" or "My Baby's Got a Cardboard Box." Both tunes involved crowd interactions. "What'd I Say," "Got My MoJo Workin'," "Turn on Your Love Light" and "Midnight Hour" made everyone perspire. As combo member Peyton Hoge said: "If you weren't sweatin', it wasn't rock 'n' roll."

Combos were often held at homes with ample driveways and large patios. Kappa Phi Fraternity President and MBA student John Farringer had one on his driveway at 2325 Golf Club Lane in the Summer of '64. Over 200 kids "boog-a-looed" to The Jaguars.

It was a great party, according to Farringer, so much so that the next day his father was seen with a broom out on the blacktop. When asked what he was doing, he related that the kids had really "gotten in to it" for there was shoe leather all over the place. Farringer said kids in those days never littered much at the homes, and beer cans were seldom seen, at least where the combos were held. That party was such a success, his sister Janice had one the next year.

Those type of fraternity and sorority parties were in abundance both in college and high school. There were eight sororities and five high-school fraternities in Nashville during those years, each having combos on a regular basis. If you add to that the school dances, kids had several choices of where to party every weekend during the school year and almost every night during the summer. It was combo craziness.

Less than a year after Farringer's combo, one was held about two miles away on the driveway at Jinx Demetrious' home on Lynnwood Boulevard. Hillsboro High student Al Battle had the misfortune of breaking in on a West High student who was dancing with Susie Stockell, Battle's classmate and my neighbor. Another West High student took exception and clocked Al with a right cross. I saw him go down in a heap as Pat Patrick and The Saturns broke off their song (which was probably "You Can't Sit Down"). The West kids peeled-out quickly. Only a brief time elapsed before the music cranked back up and kids "hully gullied" while unconscious Al was whisked away by ambulance to Vanderbilt hospital. Battle survived to do the Monkey another day.

By and large those occurrences were rare, and kids generally were well behaved. Guns were not in play during those years, only bare knuckles.

Steven Hall attended the Hillsboro High graduation combo in the summer of 1961 at Gossett's Barn, a real barn in the rear of M.T. Gossett's house on Estes Road. The Gators played for the graduates. As Hall and a couple of others walked the 100 or so yards from the barn back to their car on Estes, they came upon what seemed to be a road block, as hot rods lined both sides of the street. Friendly, unassuming Hillsboro High football player Terry "Uno" Guinn was trying to negotiate the traffic in his two-seat Volkswagen when Howard Hudgens became impatient. Not seeing Guinn's size, because of the

The Jaguars in 1964. (Lehman Keith)

small VW, Hudgens got out of his car while his girlfriend and a buddy looked on. After some verbal abuse from Hudgens, Guinn had had enough and climbed out of his vehicle, all 6 feet 3 inches, 235 pounds of him. Hall stated it looked like ten clowns exiting a minicar at the circus. Hudgens had already committed to action, and his girlfriend was watching. He hit big Terry with no effect. The retaliation, however, was dead on. Hudgens went down, then gradually got up, brushed himself off, walked back to his vehicle and drove off. Uno smiled and puttered on down the street. That was the end of that.

In addition to Gossett's Barn, people's homes, patios and driveways, there were other venues that regularly provided space for teen combos and dances: all the country clubs, the War Memorial, Skateland, The Briar Patch, Belle Meade Plaza, Calvary Methodist Teen Town, Mrs. Brown's, the Y, Dupont's the Dog House, the Sack, The Varsity Club, high school gyms, colleges and frat houses.

The Tiger-a-Go Go, Don's Den, the Uptight Club in Goodlettsville, and Willow Plunge in Franklin, The Starlight Club, Pirate's Cove, Jewish Community Center, the National Guard Armory, Cascade Plunge, the lodges and many other places hosted combo parties.

A favorite spot of the West Nashville youth was the Bellevue Skating Rink, which became known as the Chicken Coop. Just over Nine Mile Hill on Highway 70 in Bellevue, it was a rectangular structure built of "bricko block" with wire strung down the side, giving it the appearance of a chicken house. It was located atop a steep hill beneath which was an access road that served as a parking area. That road, along with Nine Mile Hill itself, was a great spot to enjoy "quality time" with your date (if you were discreet enough not to get caught, which wasn't always the case, I might add).

During band intermissions you could go back to your car and take an extra swig of Oertel's 92 or a sip of Jack, then walk back up the hill when you heard the band begin to tune up. Should you want to be fashionably late, the Warner Park Drive-In was only a mile away, or you could just go downtown to the Paramount, Tennessee or Loew's before coming out to dance.

One July Saturday night in 1964, I witnessed an enthralling dance played out at the Chicken Coop—one I had not seen demonstrated at Fortnightly, Tweensters or Nick Lambos formal dance studios. The band broke into Rufus Thomas' "The Dog" and within seconds an uninhibited, possibly inebriated, lad and lass dropped to their knees and simulated what dogs do when aroused. This was not the fox trot. The couple's synchronized rhythm moved with each line of the song—"Do the bulldog, Do the bird dog, Do the hound dog, baby." Couples in the crowd separated and formed a protective circle around the teens, as if to shield the testosterone police from witnessing the spectacle. Unlike the Gator, where one undulates with the music in a prone position, the Dog was, well, more crude. But a crowd pleaser, to say the least.

Admittedly it could get rowdy there at times. Wynne Dixon of The Saturns recalls someone tossing a beer can down his sax one night.

Things began to change with the British Invasion of 1964. The very word "combo" was phased out by the word "band." Surf music, the Beatles and eventually the psychedelic sound of the late 1960s and early '70s pushed the original rock 'n' roll sound and soul music to the side. When neighborhood schools disappeared, the word-of-mouth social marketing dried up. Drugs began invading the culture of the "flower children." The liability risks faced by homeowners hosting combos and teen spots like the Chicken Coop increased exponentially; everyone wanted to sue someone. Guns appeared. Parents became less involved.

By the late 1970s, most groups aspired to obtain recording contracts and perform in many of the new clubs that had sprung up rather than at gyms, homes and the old combo venues. Disc jockeys began playing records at parties, while fraternities and sororities became insignificant or vanished altogether. The combo experience as I knew it from 1962 to 1966 vanished.

It had been a time of social interaction, awakening of adolescence and expansion of freedom, all infused with a new kind of music brought live to us by kids we knew, met, or wanted to be like. From driveways to barns, those combos played our sound as we danced the Pony, the Fly, the Shing-a-Ling and the Mashed Potatoes.

They say the past is just that, the past. For me, I want those days, those times, those girls and that feeling to come back—but, then again, I guess I'm just a "Stubborn Kind of Fellow."

Here are some of the combo groups that energized teen "baby boomers" in the Nashville area in the 1950s and 1960s:

The Anglo Saxon (Goodlettsville)
The Argosys (Belle Meade)
The Barons
The Bubba Suggs Combo
The Casuals (with Buzz Cason, considered Nashville's first combo)
The Castaways
The Chaparrals
The Charades
The Chessmen (with Tommy VanAtta performed at the Starlight Club for almost a decade)
The Citations
The Counts of Nowhere
The Crystals (Maplewood High)
The Deltas (Gallatin area)
The Escorts (with Charlie McCoy)
The Exiles
The Exotics (with Billy Adair)
The Fabulous Beach Nutz Show Band
The Fairlanes (from Columbia)
The Gators (with Ed Hoge)
Doug Clark and the Hot Nuts
The Jades
The Jaguars (with Leo Seidner)
The Kapers (East Nashville)
King James and the Scepters
The Knight Ryders
Libido
The Majestics
The Ministers of Sound

The Monarchs (East Nashville)
The Mystic Blues
The Nashville Shadows (Glencliff High)
The Nightcaps
The New Republic
The Pivots (an all-girl group from Maplewood High later named Feminine Complex)
The Remicks
Ronnie and the Daytonas (from Hillsboro High with Lee Kraft and the Wilkins boys)
The Sands Combo
The Saturns
The Senators
The Shadows and the Pagan V (with Chip Curly)
The Shaggs (Goodlettsville)
The Silhouettes (with Howard Hudgens)
The Skipper Hunt
The Sliders (with Mac Gayden)
The Soul Searchers
The Spinners (with Jim Craig)
The Squires (who had a record produced by Lee Dorman)
The Steve Davis Group
The Taxmen
Tony and the Playboys (later The Vicars)
The Valiants (Columbia)
We the People

The Burning of the Leaves

THE FALL season during my youth was the beginning of an extended period of heightened anticipation. Summer had just ended but was hanging on long enough so that cookouts continued and all of my neighborhood friends and I could still play outside after school until darkness set in. There was crispness in the air that signaled to all that football games, family gatherings, Thanksgiving, and the holidays were not far off. Leaves started falling in October and continued accumulating on our lawn well into November. Our home on Cantrell Avenue contained large hackberry trees, several sugar maples, a couple of oaks, numerous tulip poplars, a plum tree, dogwoods, pines and others that added to the ground covering.

As far back as I can remember, my father was given the task of raking the yard and disposing of the colorful foliage. More often than not, this occurred on a Saturday or Sunday afternoon when the temperature was pleasant enough for most outdoor activities. My sisters, Beth and Lynn, would pitch in if they were not busy and would help me assist my dad with gathering the leaves into numerous piles that were scattered all around the yard. Of course, the younger I was the larger the piles looked and the larger the piles looked the more I wanted to run through or jump in them. That was half the fun. I remember many times running and jumping into the colorful hills and hiding inside, then rolling out with bits and pieces of leaves, twigs and who knows what else all over my flannel shirt, in my hair, mouth and ears.

Pictures of my sister and me collecting leaves in the fall of 1948 with a large wooden basket made it clear, at that tender young age of not quite 2, I was given proper instruction in the gathering process. The older I became the more I was called upon to help my father by taking a more substantial role

The author and his sister Lynn gathering leaves in 1948.

in the annual task. Dad's idea of a container was quite a bit different than the old crate that I was accustomed to. His was a large bed sheet or an old blanket. My mother always kept an array of frayed and tattered sheets and towels folded and stacked in the basement on top of our solid white Westinghouse washing machine. My father would lay one sheet out on the yard and use a wooden handled rake with long, metal appendages (not all even, I might add) and corral the leaves on to the sheet or blanket until it was overflowing on all sides. At that point each corner was pulled to the center and tied together with the remnants falling to the ground. He would then sling the large load over his shoulder. Depending upon how ambitious he was, the weight of the cargo could exceed a mid-sized youth. Of course, I fit the bill many times and enjoyed the ride to the dumping area submerged in the autumn collection.

Raking and carrying was just the precursor to the main event. After gathering, tying the sheet, and transporting our bounty, we would open up the bedding and release the leaves onto a brick barbecue pit that was in the corner of our backyard, next to an expansive cast-iron swing set. Our pit was built with Herbert bricks that consisted of two four-foot extensions with a complete chimney at the rear rising nearly five feet. Following an initial course in fire safety by my mom, a "strike anywhere" wooden match was used to light

This 1966 photo shows the author's nephew Vance Wheeler and nieces Amy Wheeler (left) and Kathy Wheeler dumping leaves for burning in the family barbecue pit.

some wadded-up newspapers at the very bottom of the pile. At first a small flickering light appeared, followed by some smoke, then, depending upon the moisture content of the leaves, the flames usually escalated, rapidly creating a crackling sound that emitted a small grayish cloud. Once the fire got going, it was hurry up, gather another load, carry it to the backyard from the front or side yard, and sling it on the pile. The more leaves deposited the better. You see, the flames would disappear at that point and would be replaced by a tremendous amount of smoke. These smoke clouds drifted and towered, it seemed, hundreds of feet in the air, carrying with them the smell of autumn.

Neighborhood kids were always excited by the proceedings. I remember several of us taking small sticks, poking them into the flames, stirring up the glowing embers at the bottom of the stack, and then, with the twigs burning on the end, chasing each other around the yard and shaking them in the fall air to watch the sparks fly. It was as if the 4th of July had returned.

The more leaves, the more fire and the more fire the greater the possibility that nearby vegetation would become endangered. On one occasion the flames became so high that a large ash tree located in an alley directly behind our barbequer became a cause for concern. In order to prevent the adjoining trees on the Haury's property or on "Yap" and "Pants" Herbert's property becoming a raging inferno, we quickly assembled a crack volunteer fire department consisting of several teens, an adult or two, and a handful of young children. We hurriedly attached a few sections of hose into one and stretched it all the way across the backyard and proceeded to spray the towering flames. I am sure folks passing by on Westmont Avenue believed it was a remake of a "Little Rascals" episode. The resulting smoke at that juncture was incredible. It was a successful and unintended bonus that could have resulted in a two-alarm disaster. The billowing smoke attracted a large number of youngsters who frolicked around our back yard for an extended period of time. From a distance it probably seemed a locomotive was coming down the street.

Burning and smoldering leaves with little or no wind to speak of usually made for mountainous clouds. When the wind did shift, as in a downdraft or reversal of direction, we would yell and sprint across the lawn. For us young kids, it was almost as if we were being chased by some kind of science fiction monster. It was all about the smoke and how high and far it would reach. Depending upon the direction and velocity of the wind, I wished ours would engulf most of the area and reduce visibility within the block so friends would be attracted to come play at my house. There were times a quick hop on the old gearless Schwinn bicycle was in order to see just how far the cloud bank had drifted.

The sweet, pungent aroma could usually be detected for blocks, especially on the rare occasions when Indian Summer (an unusually warm period for a fall month) occurred. Most people had room or window air-conditioning units in the 1950s or used window fans because central heat and air was almost unheard of back then. During fall warm spells, many homeowners raised the windows or turned on their fans to enjoy the unseasonable and refreshing temperature. The resulting effect was a gradual infusion of the outside air that circulated within the homes, more often than not, conjuring up thoughts that someone nearby was enjoying outside life with friends.

The burning of leaves occurred everywhere in most of the community and always in our neighborhood. It became a ritual that seemed to bring together neighbors who would stand around mesmerized by the flickering fire and aromatic warmth while wasting away the better parts of many an autumn afternoon. During cold afternoons, warming cold cheeks while facing the fire and then turning and heating the backside cheeks became an added incentive to linger around. It was as if we had our own outdoor thermostat. The flames, the accompanying smoke and the ever-present scent gave us a sense of community and a feeling that everything was okay.

We lived outside of the city of Nashville during those years and were not annexed into Metropolitan Government until the early 1960s. This inclusion into the city brought with it numerous advantages and benefits that living in the county did not have. However, there was a major drawback. The burning of the leaves continued for several more years until September 1971 when it was specifically prohibited by the Metro Health Department, division of Pollution Control. Now that we were "city folk" and therefore subject to city regulations, we were forced to comply with this new law. Many continued to disregard the ordinance until the fire department began patrolling neighborhoods, dousing fires and levying misdemeanor fines on homeowners. This decree eventually took hold and sadly marked the ending of a beloved and cherished childhood memory not only for me but also for many Nashvillians. Another part of my youth had now gone away.

Should the call of nostalgia overtake you this fall, give this suggestion a try: Get out the old two-wheeled wooden-handled push mower with exposed blades in the front (if you have one) and cut up some leaves or, just rake them into a container such as an old sheet, and carry them to a secure spot in the back yard, preferably out of sight. When the sun starts setting one pleasant fall afternoon and the wind is slight, dig a small pit or use a fireproof receptacle such as a small bucket or washtub and deposit your harvest.

Open up a lawn chair or sit on the ground. Call a couple of good friends and pour a glass of your favorite libation. Light the small pile with a "strike anywhere" wooden match. Take a sip of your beverage. Close your eyes, sniff the aroma and drift back in time to a period of youthful exuberance, of parents and siblings in the prime of life, and long-forgotten neighbors and friends not seen since.

How wonderful it is to be young again and to enjoy the burning of the leaves.

CHAPTER 24

Westerns and Cowboys

To save my soul I can't get a date,
Baby's got it turned on channel eight.
Now Wyatt Earp and the Big Cheyenne
They're comin' thru the T.V. shootin' up the land.
Ah…um…my baby loves the Western movies,
Bam, bam, shoot 'em up Pow.
Ah…um…my baby loves the Western movies.
—The Olympics, "Western Movies" (1958)

IN THE early 1950s I couldn't get a date either. I wasn't even 10 at that time. But I was ready to watch western movies, which peaked in the 1940s and 1950s. Cowboys were the kings of radio, the silver screen and later television, and were idolized by kids like me. Our imagination was captivated by these men with 10-gallon hats, flashy scarves, leather chaps and shiny spurs who rode atop galloping horses with their blazing six shooters chasing Indians, cattle rustlers and bad guys across dusty plains and around huge tumbleweeds.

History tells us that in 1890 the Census Bureau announced it would no longer track westward migration. By then the west had been divided up and populated to the point where a frontier line no longer existed. But the tales of those westward-moving folks would continue to be written by authors and even by the settlers themselves. So much so that at the inception of cinema there were hundreds of stories about the west readily available to filmmakers. The movies were cheap, easy to make, and our culture was already familiar with Buffalo Bill, Wyatt Earp, Wild Bill Hickock and the like. In 1903—some

50 years prior to my donning a cowboy belt with those metallic, toy six shooters filled with rolls of paper caps—Thomas Edison came out with a movie titled "The Great Train Robbery." Lasting only 12 minutes, with no sound, it set off another frontier movement—the western movie.

My first recollection of seeing a western picture show was probably at the Paramount or the Tennessee Theater. It

The author (first boy on left) is pictured at the Franklin Rodeo in 1953 along with neighborhood friends, Josh Ambrose and Rhea Sumpter, and Cowboy "Cactus" Close of Lafayette, Ga.

was in 3D, which meant you had to wear those large, black, circular spectacles. It was in 1953, and the movie featured cowboy legend Guy Madison in "The Charge at Feather River," acclaimed as one of the best Indian-vs.-Calvary movies ever made. All I remember as a 6-year-old were the Indian arrows coming straight at me, causing me to duck on a regular basis. The entire movie was a spectacle to me.

"Hondo," with John Wayne, came out that year as well and was also filmed in 3D. Westerns seemed to dominate the theaters in the late 1940s and early 1950s. Everyone knew the top stars, such as World War II hero Audie Murphy and the legends like Wayne, Randolph Scott, Gary Cooper, Alan Ladd, as well as old-time stars like Hoot Gibson and the first big cowboy from the silent era, Tom Mix.

Just a few of the westerns that entertained us in 1953-1954 at the movies were: the classic "High Noon"; "The Stand at Apache River" was at the Fifth Avenue; "War Arrow" with screen favorite Jeff Chandler and Maureen O'Hara debuted at Loew's; Gary Cooper starred in "Blowing Wild" at the Melrose; Robert Taylor and Ava Gardner graced the screen in "Ride, Vaquero" at the

The author's sisters, Lynn and Beth, are dressed up in cowgirl outfits in 1940, illustrating the popularity of western movies even before television.

Belmont; Johnny Mack Brown kept the peace in "Texas Law Men" at the Capitol while Rod Cameron fought for the country in "Calvary Scout" showing at the Woodland. Singing cowboy Gene Autry introduced us to what life was like in "The Old West" at the Woodbine Theater.

Joining that stampede were the drive-ins. "Seminole" featuring Rock Hudson played the Skyway and Montague at the same time Audie Murphy shot his way through "Gunsmoke" at the Crescent on Thompson Lane. Not to be outdone, the Colonial lit up the night with "Red Mountain" and Alan Ladd. There was rarely a time when a western was not showing somewhere. It was a good time to be a fan.

In 1950 the popularity of the cowboy and his lifestyle, along with an idea of a fundraising project, led the Franklin Rotary Club to start a huge tradition in Franklin, Tenn., simply called the Franklin Rodeo. As he knew my fondness for westerns, my father took me and a couple of neighborhood kids to the 1953 event held at the County Center. Part of that year's Review Appeal article stated: "All the color, action and excitement of the 'Wild' West roars into Franklin this Friday night and Saturday afternoon.... Some of the nation's finest rodeo performers are expected to give the crowd a real show for their money.... Bronc riding will be the first feature of the very splendid program. Some 'real salty' animals have been brought here to test the ability of the of bronc busters."

In addition there was a quarter-horse show, calf roping, barrel races,

This lobby card for the 1953 movie "The Charge at Feather River" touts its 3D presentation. The author saw the film at age 6 and mainly remembers dodging arrows.

bulldogging, calf scramble, ribbon roping and bull riding on Brahma bulls (my favorite). Pre-rodeo parades snaked down Main Street, and the annual rodeo barbeque supper and bingo was held at the local swimming hole, Willow Plunge.

To top off the day we had our picture made with a "real" cowboy, Cactus Close of Lafayette, Ga. Looking at that snapshot later I thought I might not want to be left alone with this guy.

A few years later, around 1959 or 1960, several Franklin High and Battle Ground Academy students—many of them "highly motivated"—were heard mulling over the idea of riding one of the bulls being kept in pens adjacent to where the cowboys hitched up their trailers. As the teens gathered around the bullpen, one of them heard a commotion, as if the beasts were escaping. Deciding that whatever the noise was, it was not a good thing, he and a friend got out of there and wandered off to the high school gathering spot on Lewisburg Pike called the Gilco.

From a source familiar with the incident: "The next morning the word was out that somebody had turned the bulls out on the Natchez area, and bulls were all over the place, scaring everyone! The police and the Fowlkes brothers spent all night gathering them up. Many [people] were angry!"

I would guess so. Thank goodness the Releasing of the Bulls never became an annual rite.

"Out of the clear blue of the western sky comes SKY KING!" This was the opening salvo of the "Sky King" television show on Saturdays. Television gradually became a huge media outlet, and many former theater greats and radio stars, such as Sky King, made the transition. The series ran from 1951 to 1962 and featured Sky with his big, wide

"High Noon," a Western movie starring Gary Cooper, was released in 1952.

hat gliding out of the Flying Crown Ranch in Arizona piloting Songbird, his Cessna 310B aircraft. Along with his cute little niece Penny (the boys' favorite) and his nephew Clipper, King captured bad guys and found lost hikers every weekend.

As the "William Tell Overture" played in the background, announcer Fred Foy's voice came on the air: "A fiery horse with speed of light, a cloud of dust and hearty Hi-yo, Silver! The Lone Ranger, with his faithful Indian companion, Tonto, the daring and resourceful masked rider of the plains led the fight for law and order in the early western United States. Nowhere in the pages of history can one find a greater champion of justice. Return with us now to those thrilling days of yesteryear. From out of the past come the thundering hoofbeats of the great horse Silver. The Lone Ranger rides again!" From 1949 to 1957, Clayton Moore, John Hart and Jay Silverheels (a full-bloodied Mohawk) rode the plains of the west on Silver and Scout as we watched

in black and white. He never killed anyone, never kissed the girl, never drank, cussed or smoked. Neither did he accept reward money nor show his face to anyone other than faithful Tonto, and he always upheld a moral code and respected the rights and beliefs of others. This was not unlike many of the long-running television western stars of the day. "Hi-yo, Silver. Away!" Who was that masked man?

Roy Rogers and his horse Trigger pose for a photo to publicize his television program "The Roy Rogers Show," which aired from 1951 to 1957.

One of the most popular westerns to air on the small screen featured the King of the Cowboys, Roy Rogers, and his wife, the Queen of the Cowgirls, Dale Evans, on "The Roy Rogers Show," which was seen from 1951 to 1957. Roy's horse, Trigger, was dubbed the "Smartest Horse in the Movies." Evans's ride was Buttermilk, and along with their German Shepherd dog, Bullet, they all resided at the Double R ranch with sidekick Pat Brady and his Jeep, Nellybelle. They tried to maintain law and order at their diner and in the town of Mineral City. It aired both on WSM Channel 4 and on WSIX Channel 8. Roy's "Riders Club Rules" stated the following:

1. Be neat and clean
2. Be courteous and polite
3. Always obey your parents
4. Protect the weak and help them
5. Be brave but never take chances

6. Study hard and learn all you can

7. Be kind to animals and take care of them

8. Eat all your food and never waste any

9. Believe God and go to Sunday School regularly

10. Always respect our flag and our country.

Roy and Dale's duet, "Happy Trails," was one of those closing theme songs you had trouble getting out of your head:

> *Happy Trails to you, until we meet again.*
> *Happy trails to you, keep smilin' until then.*
> *Just sing a song and bring the sunny weather.*
> *Happy trails to you, until we meet again.*

Gene Autry, another singing cowboy from radio and movies, along with Tex Ritter, made the move to TV as well. Autry rode Champion and was assisted in bad guy roundups with sidekicks Chill Wills and Fuzzy Knight (Sagebrush), and in the movies with western comic Smiley Burnett, better known as Frog Millhouse. Those sidekicks added levity to the gunplay. At the top of my list was the grizzled Gabby Hayes. I can still hear him utter the lines: "Consarn it!," "dagnabbitt" and "Why you gol durned whippersnapper." He became Roy Rogers' sidekick, but for most of his movie days he rode the plains with Hopalong Cassidy out of the Bar 20 ranch. Edgar Buchanan played Red Connors as his TV accomplice.

Hopalong Cassidy (William Boyd) and his gorgeous white horse, Topper, were sponsored by Post cereal (Sugar Crisp and the like): "Candy coated puffed wheat the whole family will go for. Now let's ride the range with Hopalong Cassidy!" Hoppy (as we called him) was described as a man of action, sworn enemy of crime and cruelty, epitome of gallantry and fair play with a strong sense of justice and highly-regarded family values. He became so popular 15,000 letters deluged his empire on a weekly basis. He was one of the good guys who did not wear a white hat. His trademark black 10-gallon fedora was unique. Like most television stars his name was put on everything. I had a Hopalong Cassidy tin lunch box I carried to school. There were bicycles, t-shirts, baseball bats, toy guns, holsters, watches, radios, comic books and BB guns. There was even Hoppyland Amusement Park near Los Angeles. He covered it all. In 1950, Time magazine described Hoppy as someone who "did not smoke, drink or kiss girls, who tried to capture the rustlers instead of shooting them, and who always let the villain draw first if gunplay was inevitable."

Boyd himself said: "I played down the violence, tried to make Hoppy an admirable character, and I insisted on grammatical English." This guy didn't sing, dance, play team sports, tennis or race cars.

This "Hopalong Cassidy" comic book was published in 1949. The character also appeared in movies and on television and radio.

Good thing I was not offered the role.

B-grade westerns ruled Saturday viewing for us kids. It seemed to me that the posse would chase the culprits through the same pass and around the same huge rock week after week. The ping sounds those bullets made careening off of boulders never changed either. The familiar galloping of hooves and blowing tumbleweeds became iconic along with names of many of those stars. There was Lash LaRue, Sunset Carson, the lonely cowboy Tex Fletcher, Tim McCoy, James Ellison and Dusty King.

Our local stations even had cowboy hosts. There was Cowboy Bill on Channel 5 and Ruffin Reddy on Channel 4 (see "Kid's TV" in the March 2012 issue of The Nashville Retrospect). Westerns became so popular that on Saturdays in 1954 WSIX 8 started with a double feature at 9:30 a.m. and ended at 1:30 p.m. with "Saturday Westerns." At 10:30 a.m. WLAC 5 aired "Tales of the Texas Rangers," and from noon until 2 p.m. it was Roy Rogers followed by Gene Autry. WSM 4 broadcast "Buffalo Bill, Jr." and Roy Rogers again until 6 p.m. Even kiddie favorite Howdy Doody was dressed with bandana, jeans and boots. His partner was called Buffalo Bob.

Those TV westerns of yesterday were legendary. Some of the other ones I watched that started in the 1950s included:

• "The Cisco Kid"—"Hey, Cisco. Hey, Poncho...";

• "Wild Bill Hickock"—Guy Madison on Buckshot with gravelly-voiced Jingles P. Jones (Andy Devine) aboard Joker;

• "Kit Carson"—With Mexican sidekick El Toro;

• "The Range Rider"—Jock Mahoney;

• "Death Valley Days"—Stanley "Old Ranger" Andrews and later Ronald Reagan as hosts. Sponsored by 20 Mule Team Borax;

• "Annie Oakley"—Gail Davis on her horse Target and sidekick "Tag" Hawkins with Pixie;

A poster for the 1953 movie "The Stand at Apache River."

• "Gunsmoke"—Probably the most popular of all time. Matt Dillon rode on his horse Buck;

• "Cheyenne"—Last name of Bodie. Muscular Clint Walker in the role;

• "Tales of Wells Fargo"—Dale Robertson on Jubilee with William Demarest as Jeb;

• "Have Gun Will Travel"—"Hey, boy. Hey, girl..." Came on the same night as "Gunsmoke" and starred Richard Boone as Paladin. He had a famous business card;

• "Wagon Train"—Ward Bond was in charge;

- "Maverick"—A Sunday-night favorite featuring James Garner and Jack Kelly among others;
- "Colt .45"—Wade Preston as Chris Colt;
- "Wyatt Earp"—Hugh O'Brian;
- "Wanted Dead or Alive"—Legendary Steve McQueen as Josh Randall;
- "The Rifleman"—Chuck Connors as Lucas McCain;
- "The Lawman"—John Russell;
- "Rawhide"—Eric Fleming as Gil Favor, Clint Eastwood as Rowdy Yates and Sheb Wooley as Pete Nolan the Scout;
- "Bonanza"—Lorne Green was Pa, Hoss Cartwright was Dan Blocker, Michael Landon played Little Joe, and Pernell Roberts was Adam;
- "Laramie"—John Smith starred as Slim Sherman;
- "The Rebel"—Johnny Yuma played by Nick Adams. "Johnny Yuma... was a Rebel"; and
- "Bat Masterson"—Gene Barry with that cane and top hat.

Westerns as I knew them began disappearing in the late 1960s as color was added to most everything produced. The old, standard black-and-white became a thing of the past. The mood of the country was changing, too, and no longer was it clearly laid out as just a "good guy vs. bad guy" world where the good always triumphed over evil.

Westerns showcased men who were tough and chivalrous, possessing a mentality of "pull yourself up by your bootstraps." You were either a man or a coward. It was the wilderness, horses and guns. They had real meaning.

But those stories of the old west and pioneering eventually became stale, and most of the famous western stars passed on. The "goody-goody stuff" of Roy Rogers and Hopalong Cassidy became unmarketable. The mystique of the frontier had faded as the population had ballooned across the Mississippi. As long as folks could envision the west as an open land of adventure, the western stayed relevant, but by the 1960s those days had slipped too far into the past. The iconic cowboys and their trusty sidekicks of the mid-20th century rode off on those faithful steeds and disappeared into the sunset. With them went a wholesome facet of our lives, never to return.

As for me, corralling another Hopalong Cassidy lunchbox on store shelves is impossible...consarnit dagnabbitt!

CHAPTER 25

The Happiness Club

TONY SUDEKUM had an idea that by constructing a movie theater in his front yard, at 4301 Harding Pike, it would fill a much needed entertainment void for the growing number of families moving into the surrounding neighborhood. I also feel sure he had no idea of what the lasting impression such a venue would have on the kids who would patronize his creation.

The Belle Meade Theater opened on Wednesday, May 1, 1940, at 6:45 p.m. with the showing of "Charlie McCarthy, Detective." A newspaper ad cited "Spacious Free Parking for our Patrons, Featuring Leon Cole at the Hammond Novachord and Tim Sanders in a Special Radiocast." Prices ranged from 10 to 30 cents.

Belle Meade Theater Manager E. J. Jordon from a 1940 Nashville Banner photograph. (Nashville Public Library, Nashville Room)

At a cost of $250,000, the Marr and Holman building featured over 1,600 lights on the outside. A 75-foot tower, topped off by a huge crystal ball, rose from a curved marquee under which was the ticket booth and surrounding walls of Georgia marble and porcelain. The inside had a marvelous, wood-veneer, railed stairway leading to the balcony. Its proscenium stage looked out over 1,200 seats, some double-sized, that led to a stainless

From the June 10, 1948, Nashville Banner: "Nearly 2,000 members of the Belle Meade Theater Happiness Club turned out Saturday afternoon to greet E. J. Jordan, manager of the theater, at his birthday party. Jordan is pictured center, rear, surrounded by a few hundred of the children as they poured into the theater to view the stage show presented by students of the Elizabeth Bryant Combs Studios and the film feature. All members of the Happiness Club, restricted to children between the ages of five and 15, were guests of the manager at the party which has been an annual event for the past several years." (Nashville Public Library, Nashville Room)

steel and mirrored foyer with large rounded windows. The electrical display of the theater was described in "Boxoffice" magazine as "rivaling anything shown at the New York World's Fair and will probably be considered the most unusual thing ever presented to the public in connection with a theatre. ... It may well be the belle of all southern movie houses."

Edwin Jeffries Jordan, a native Tennessean, was chosen as the manager. He was formerly with the National Beauty Pageant Association in Kansas City, Mo., but acquired his entertainment acumen as a vaudeville magician touring with the legendary Blackstone.

On opening night, Jordan welcomed screen stars Irene Dunne, Randolph Scott, producer Hal Roach and Leo McCarey. Dunne noticed a piece of marble left by a workman and inquired as to what it was for. E. J. gave her a pen, and she signed it along with the others. The famous Belle Meade Theater

Wall of Fame was born. Throughout the years over 200 celebrities made their marks, including Walt Disney, Bob Hope, Bing Crosby, Andy Griffith, Fess Parker, Roy Rogers, Ronald Reagan, Charlton Heston and Dinah Shore. It became as famous as the Hollywood Walk of Fame during its time.

On Saturday, May 4, just three days after the opening, Jordan's entertaining background surfaced. He passed the word in the neighborhood that all kids would be admitted for free. Thirty-two showed up for the western "South of the Border" starring Gene Autry, accompanied by cartoons, short subjects and the serial "The Green Hornet." Word circulated fast among local kids that the theater was the place to be on Saturday afternoons. A vast array of goodies were prevalent at the concessions and the cost was cheap. Kids had such a great time the manager decided to name the Saturday afternoon funfest, The Happiness Club. Membership was very rigorous. It required you to be from ages 5 to 15 and make three visits.

Shortly after its inception, Jordan conducted auditions for stage acts to entertain the kids. Later Miss Barbara Freeman took over that role in addition to providing music on her finely-tuned piano. Local school children with vocal skills, tap-dancing talents and other stage abilities were recruited.

In 1943, a 6-year-old neighborhood kid, Robert Webb, was taken by his mother to meet Mr. Jordan and to "try out" for The Happiness Club stage show. Webb was a gifted soprano at a very young age and was recognized as such at Woodmont School and in the community. The pudgy, bespeckled, bucktoothed youngster made his first Happiness Club stage appearance with the "Anniversary Song," which he later said was not an appropriate number for the setting of hundreds of grade school children. He had been taught the song by his mother and knew all the words by heart, hence his selection. Scared, he walked robotically from backstage to the stationary microphone. With his mom on piano he began to sing:

> Oh, how we danced on the night we were wed
> We vowed our true love, though a word wasn't said
> The world was in bloom, there were stars in the skies
> Except for the few that were there in your eyes.

Fortunately, one of the rules of the club was no booing of the acts. As a result Webb received a thunderous applause. He became a regular later, singing more relevant tunes such as Big Band numbers and Sinatra songs, and Jordan started referring to him as "Little Frankie." He even went on to perform for Ted Mack at a huge show at Nashville's War Memorial in 1954.

Seven-year-old Bobby Russell made his Happiness Club debut with a variety of, as Webb said, "unrecognizable bird calls." The clueless audience nonetheless thought it sounded great. The red-headed Russell and Webb performed in tandem on numerous occasions. Bobby went on to write the famous "Little Green Apples" in later years. Also gracing the stage at the Happiness Club was 10-year-old Pat Boone, who went on to become a mega recording star. Jordan nicknamed him "Little Bing."

As membership increased, Mr. Jordan devised a schedule complete with rules. The first 30 minutes were basically a kid's dream come true: Screaming, running up and down the aisles and putting your feet on the back of the theater seats were all allowed, as long as you were enjoying yourself. Jordan once said that during this time on Saturday afternoon it was requested that attending parents should not disturb the children. This was great fun and could best be described as a chaotic free-for-all.

After this bedlam subsided, Jordan would take the mic and, with a bouncing ball appearing over each word on the screen, lead the throng in singing the theme song, "Happy Days Are Here Again." It went like this:

Happy Days are here again
The skies above are clear again
So let's sing a song of cheer again
Happy Days are here again
Altogether shout it now
There's no one who can doubt it now
So let's tell the world about it now
Happy Days are here again
Your cares and troubles are gone
There'll be no more from now on, from now on
Happy Days are here again.

Once the theme had been sung, all of the kids who had birthdays during the week had their names announced and were summoned to the stage. He always gave them a free treat at the concession stand. In addition, prizes were awarded each week. You kept half of your ticket stub in hopes the matching number would be called. As for the prizes, I don't recollect what they were but suspected that some were to be redeemed at Moon Drugs, which was next door, and a big part of the entire proceedings (Clyde Moon was a big supporter of all the neighbor-

From the March 2, 1954, Nashville Banner: "Nine-year-old Judy Bobo, daughter of Mr. and Mrs. James Bobo, filled the bill as tap dance artist during the entertainment portion of the Happiness Club meeting. The pianist is Miss Barbara Freeman, who auditions talent as well as accompanying acts." (Nashville Public Library, Nashville Room, photo by Jack Gunter)

hood kids—see Chapter 20). Certain rules then would be emphasized, such as not throwing popcorn, no booing the acts and no unruly behavior such as had already taken place. Then the show began.

My sister Beth recollects it was the destination for all grammar school kids who could come up with the nickel to get in. Between the age of 12 and 14 in the late 1940s, she and her friends would walk the seven to eight blocks from our house on Cantrell down to the Belle Meade Theater to go to The Happiness Club. The mirrors on the ceiling of the lobby, the wonderful curved staircase to the balcony (which was off limits to Happiness Club members) and the wall of photos were great attractions for preteen girls, who in turn were attractions for preteen boys. Westerns were the big features, usually starring Hopalong Cassiddy, Gene Autry, Roy Rogers and the like with the serials or "cliff-hangers" being the most popular. They would abruptly end with the hero in grave peril, often dangling from a cliff or seemingly facing death in a car that had wrecked and exploded. It kept you coming back each week to see what happened. It was clever marketing.

When the price went from 5 to 12 cents, those who did not have a big enough allowance for admission, popcorn and candy created an uproar. Mr. Jordan, however, never denied anyone admission. He would always give in to those whose funds were inadequate.

Beth said she received 25 cents a week, so she made it okay. Young Bob Webb and his brother were always given 25 cents to divide between them for the Saturday afternoon club. Bob's brother, Elkin, was 8 in 1944. Being one year older he became the holder of the quarter. Costing 12 cents each to get in left 1 cent for candy. On one particular occasion while waiting in line to enter, Elkin decided he was keeping the penny. Little Frankie snapped and attacked his brother. Girls screamed, clothes ripped, buttons popped and fists flew as the two siblings went at it. Mr. Jordan heard the ruckus, grabbed both boys by the collars and scolded young Bob about his behavior. He did not know young Elkin at the time but later learned of the connection. Mrs. Webb was called and her disappointment resulted in a stern tongue-lashing and switching. Ironically, Elkin later became a respected usher at the theater.

Jordan once said: "A child psychologist would find a fertile field for research here. Children save some of their best tricks for the movie." He always encouraged honesty, not that it always mattered to some. One kid, upon being admitted, would go to the fire exit and let in his buddies. Another resembled an old-time medicine man as he stood on a wooden box at the end of the ticket line calling for donations for another kid that supposedly had lost his money. An even bolder move took place when an enterprising youngster went up and down the aisles collecting money from everyone, saying "Give me two cents." No cause was given. For some reason most complied with the demanding request.

Jordan recalled, in a news article in 1954, that a 5-year-old little girl would come up and ask him for 2 cents for some candy every Saturday. He gladly gave it to her and would add a nickel if he had it, only to find out later she was giving the same treatment to all the ushers. Her pockets and stomach were both filled by the time the show ended.

Despite all the chicanery and mischievousness no one was ever prohibited from coming to the show, especially for lack of funds. In fact, Mr. Jordan regularly invited kids from St. Mary's orphanage and local hospitals to come for no charge. He also held an annual event on his birthday inviting all kids to be his guest at The Happiness Club. In 1948 his birthday

From the March 2, 1954, Nashville Banner: "Check this picture of solid comfort. The lounging gentleman is Jay Wallace, seven-and-one-half-year old son of Mr. and Mrs. James E. Wallace of Lynwood Terrace. He knows he's safe because there's no rule against putting your feet on the seats during the 'Happiness Club.'" (Nashville Public Library, Nashville Room, photo by Jack Gunter)

bash attracted an amazing 2,000 club members (see photo on page 167). Admission was free as was the ice cream.

I, of course, was a regular attendee and member, beginning in the mid-1950s. My friends and I would either walk or ride bikes the half-mile or so, and if riding, park in the multi-slotted steel rack that sat under the marquee. As I aged into double figures, the acts continued to be tap dancing and local vocals as well as serials, cartoons and features. I was especially fond of the "Merrie Melodies" cartoons for some reason, probably because it was a mystery as to what character would be shown. However, the features during this period had changed from westerns to science fiction and monster flicks. The atomic era was in full swing and a number of movies played on that fear. In 1959, The Happiness Club showcased a movie titled "The Hideous Sun Demon." It was a low-budget film centering around a scientist whose radiation experiment malfunctioned and caused him to turn into a giant lizard when the sun came out. I think producers learned never to include the word "hideous" in the title after that.

Mr. Jordan on this occasion had a special treat in store for us. Just prior to the start of this sci-fi gem, the lights went out and a spotlight from the balcony silhouetted some tall person on stage dressed as Boris Karloff's monster in the movie "Frankenstein." The kids in the first few rows screamed, especially the little girls, as the look-alike made grunting sounds and walked across the stage and down the steps with hands raised in a grisly manner. I can only assume that Mr. Jordan expected the some 1,200 kids to huddle together and shriek in horror as the "monster" made his way up the middle isle. Much to his chagrin, the older members (me included) were not the least bit frightened.

I did not start it, but shortly after he slowly ascended past the third row one could see small objects hurtling towards him highlighted by the tremendous wattage of the spotlight. By the time the imposter got to row five his hands had become shields protecting him from an unbelievable barrage of Raisonettes, Goobers, Juicy Fruits, Milk Duds, partially chewed Black Jack and Teaberry gum and half-eaten Sugar Daddies on a stick. Cowering from the onslaught, he retreated and disappeared through the side exit to howls and cheers of the youngsters.

Seconds later E. J. emerged as all the theater lights came on. With stern words he threatened to shut down the program for the afternoon if the unruly behavior did not cease. Order was finally restored. The monster, I am sure, received much needed first aid, and we all witnessed the hideousness of the sun demon.

December 1961 hit hard as my Happiness Club membership expired. Age 15 came too soon for a lot of us. Mr. Jordan continued to provide wholesome acts and movies for youngsters until 1968 when he retired due to an illness. E. J. was a stern but loving man, one who knew not only all the kids by name but the grown-ups as well. He would even phone his regulars when he thought a film might be to their liking, and would likewise advise them when a feature was playing he felt would not be worth their time. He would always greet movie-goers as they entered and as they left saying "Good night and come again." He was a unique and caring person of the "Popcorn Circuit" who happened to be a manager of a wonderful neighborhood theater. He still made appearances for a few more years in his wheelchair until he passed away in

1973. The paper said "An Era of Theater Showmanship Ended—Unequalled in Nashville."

That unique period of time is now gone, as is the theater. It closed Feb. 28, 1991, leaving only the name on the towering marquee. The Wall of Fame photos and marble slab are in storage at the Tennessee State Museum awaiting funds for display.

What are not gone are the everlasting memories etched in the souls of thousands of adults who were once young kids who spent their Saturday afternoons at Tony Sudekum's fabulous Belle Meade Theater as members of Edwin Jeffries Jordan's Happiness Club. To take a few lines of the theme song of one of the Wall of Fame's iconic signers, Bob Hope:

Thanks for the memory,
Of things I can't forget …
How lucky I was!

CHAPTER 26

From Vietnam to Memphis

If you are going to San Francisco,
Be sure to wear some flowers in your hair.
—Scott McKenzie, "San Francisco" (1967)

IT WAS a favorite song of the G.I.s in Vietnam in 1968 and was played by Vietnamese bands performing for troops like me wishing to get back home, albeit without flowers in my hair. Most every soldier returning from Southeast Asia would land in San Francisco after a yearlong tour of duty, hence the popularity. I vowed to never miss another Christmas with my wife and family and had a picture taken just to remind me of what it was like in that far away place during the holiday.

My 13-hour, medicated flight landed me not in San Fran but in Seattle, in driving rain. Like most of my fellow soldiers, I envisioned at least a few flags waving for a job well done. Not to be. We were greeted by a few long-haired protestors.

The author poses for a Christmas photo in 1968 while serving in Vietnam.

After a brief wait in the Army barracks, where I intentionally left my duffle bag of military belongings, I was transferred to a flight bound for Houston where I was to be flown back to my new bride and family in Nashville. Being dressed in full uniform garnered no respect as I was "bumped" off my flight. If not for the benevolence of an Army vet who bought me a drink at the bar, the experience would have been extremely disappointing. Finally, with help from my father, I was placed on a mail-carrier flight that landed in Nashville in the wee morning hours in the last full week of January 1969. Home at last.

The author and his wife, Carolyn, after moving to an apartment in Memphis in August 1969. The No. 13 apartment was the only one available in the complex.

After a short leave, my wife, Carolyn, and I set off in our 1968 Volkswagen for Fitzsimmons Hospital in Aurora, Col., where I would finish out my military obligation. During off-duty hours there we rode motorcycles, went to local parks, threw Frisbees, visited the mountains, ice skated and collapsed the double bed furnished by the apartment complex. I also blew out the back window of our car with a CO_2 pellet gun one afternoon in a forgettable moment.

Still being a fan of the horror shows, one night I subjected Carolyn to a "Dracula" marathon featuring Christopher Lee and Peter Cushing at the New East 70 Drive-In Theater. We didn't get home until 2:30 am.

One week after Sonny Liston knocked out Scrap Iron Johnson for the heavyweight title, on May 24, I separated from the Army. After the long trip back to Nashville, a new beginning got underway on June 2. God bless my folks, for not only did they look after a Thai student named Suri for a couple of years, they also allowed us to occupy my old room for the next several months.

It was back to Peabody College for the wife, to try to graduate in the summer, while I enrolled in, of all things, a Botany class. Color blindness and the inability to tell the difference between a pin oak and a redbud made it a challenge. Field trips to Marrowbone Lake to take in the foliage were really not my thing. Joe Cocker's 1968 "I Get by with a Little Help from My Friends" was an appropriate theme song there.

When not in school I played basketball and foolishly turned down an offer to suit up for Lipscomb (too strict for me at the time). I enjoyed backyard whiffle ball, hit golf balls at West Meade Driving Range and on local courses, and participated in softball games at Hillsboro High School with old acquaintances. During one of our games former Burro Lenny Celauro noticed

some "hippies" taking pictures of graffiti painted on the façade of the gym. He climbed up to the top and changed "Piss on Earth" to "Mars or Bust." God bless Lenny. All I painted was a friend's rental property, my mother-in-law's garage on Draughon Avenue and my penny loafers.

We swam at the Hathcock pool and at the new Swim N' Sun on White Bridge Road. We ate at our favorite haunts, watched movies around town, and posed for pictures on my mother's patio with her once-a-year bloomer, the Night

The author poses with the family's Night Blooming Cereus in 1969.

Blooming Cereus. In July we took a trip to Monteagle Mountain for a weekend. The highlight there was my brother-in-law vomiting in a 50-gallon trash drum behind the first tee at the hillside golf course in Sewanee. His heave caused an errant shot by an elderly gentleman. I made sure he never forgot it. It was "good times," as they say.

Back in Nashville we frequented our favorite spots, many of which would soon disappear. Vester's in Green Hills had a bowling machine that was a big attraction. Rick Chambers provided us with free admission where he worked, a downtown watering

PIZZAS

To Avoid Errors Please Order By The Numbers Listed Below

1. PLAIN (CHEESE AND SAUCE)	13. PEPPERONI
2. CHEDDAR CHEESE	14. HAM
3. GARLIC	15. BACON
4. ONION	16. HOT GREEN PEPPERS
5. GREEN PEPPER	17. BLACK OLIVE
6. WINE	18. SPANISH OLIVE
7. GROUND BEEF	19. MUSHROOM
8. ITALIAN SAUSAGE (GROUND)	20. ANCHOVIES
9. ITALIAN SALAMI	21. CRAB MEAT
10. SALAMI	22. SHRIMP
11. VIENNA SAUSAGE	23. LOBSTER
12. CANADIAN BACON	24. ITALIAN PEPPERS

EXTRA CHEESE WILL BE PRICED AS AN ADDITIONAL INGREDIENT

THE ELLIS SPECIAL

A LIGHT BLEND OF SEVEN INGREDIENTS FOR THE PIZZA GOURMET'S PALATE!

GROUND BEEF — BACON — MUSHROOMS — ONIONS
SPANISH OLIVES — HOT GREEN PEPPERS — PEPPERONI
(No substitutions will be made)

	Small	Medium	Large
	$2.85	$4.15	$5.15

THE FARE

	SMALL 9"	MEDIUM 12"	LARGE 15"	
PLAIN CHEESE # 1	$ 1.15	$ 1.90	$ 2.70	
1 INGREDIENT	$ 1.65	$ 2.65	$ 3.35	PRICES DO NOT
2 INGREDIENTS	$ 2.05	$ 3.15	$ 3.95	INCLUDE
3 INGREDIENTS	$ 2.45	$ 3.65	$ 4.55	STATE SALES TAX
4 INGREDIENTS	$ 2.85	$ 4.15	$ 5.15	
5 INGREDIENTS	$ 3.25	$ 4.65	$ 5.75	
6 INGREDIENTS	$ 3.65	$ 5.15	$ 6.35	
7 INGREDIENTS	$ 4.05	$ 5.65	$ 6.95	

ALL PIZZAS MADE ½ AND ½ ARE PRICED ACCORDING TO THE SIDE WITH THE MOST INGREDIENTS. EXAMPLE: (SMALL) ½ NO. 8 AND ½ NO. 19-13 IS PRICED $2.05.

A House of Pizza menu from 1969. The restaurant, located at 27 White Bridge Road, also served spaghetti, lasagna and minestrone.

hole called The Landing. Lum's at the Highway 70/100 split was a regular stop; their famous hot dogs and the "Lumburger" always met expectations.

My favorite pizza spot was Ellis Levine's House of Pizza at 27 White Bridge Road. The menu even offered six-packs to go. I spent many hours in the Keg Room downstairs enduring Reed Majors' rendition of Jose Feliciano's hit "Light My Fire" while scarfing down the Ellis Special. (Back in high school my neighbor Dave's mother would raise hell with him when she would enter his odorous room on a Saturday morning after we devoured one of those delights. Her comment: "I don't mind you and Tommy drinking that much, just lay off the onion and garlic pizza." It was a poor cover-up attempt.)

A block or two away from the House of Pizza, the Hounds Tooth at 103 White Bridge featured champagne specials for the sophisticated set and promoted Capt. Bill Kelsey and the Whalers for entertainment. Their slogan was questionable: "Do you have Demophobia?" The word means "a fear of crowds," which either indicated a quiet atmosphere or that no one ever came.

Some three miles away, on Abbott Martin Road, the Roundup was no second-rate joint either. Mismanagement, just like at the House of Pizza, eventually spelled its demise.

For a nice night out, the wife and I would go to our "getaway" restaurant, Kinnard's on 21st Avenue. The steaks and atmosphere were top notch, as were the buffalo meat and corn cakes at our anniversary eatery, Nero's Cactus Canyon. College and high school kids continued to make the drive out Highway 41 to Smyrna to a Polynesian diner called The Omni Hut. Its slogan was "Created in a Million Miles of Travel."

The Dobbs House and the Albert Pick Motel made our list while the Shoney's, famous during the drive-in craze, offered the "Half Pound O' Ground Round" at cut-rate prices. We regularly went with family to the famous Cross Keys in Green Hills Village. Minnie Pearl, Eddy Arnold and KFC had chicken chains while the Burger Chef and The Flaming Steer always had a deal. Dipper Dan Ice Cream was nearby and provided a tasty alternative.

Those few months in the middle of 1969 also entailed shopping at Zayre, Karl's Shoes, and Casual Corner in Belle Meade. There were many trips to Buckley's Record Shop on Church and to the "dime stores" like Woolworth's, Kuhns' Variety and the Ben Franklin 5 and 10. Nashville Extra Value Days were going strong, with 175 stores participating. A 1969 Nash Rambler sold for the hefty sum of $1,869. Harveys sold men's shirts for $2.44, and girls panties for $.48. I passed on those.

We took in many movies at venues soon to vanish. One night at the House of Pizza with friends, we heard rumors that a car-crash scene was to be filmed downtown for an upcoming flick. Off everyone went to see the spectacle at 13th and Church Street. An added attraction was to catch a glimpse of the appealing Yvette Mimieux, who was the star heroine. The movie, "The Delta Factor," opened a year later in Nashville on May 15, 1970.

The crash involved a sports car demolishing a makeshift telephone booth and careening into a service station, shattering its glass window. Four to five blocks were barricaded off. Just prior to the filming one civilian attempted to use the telephone booth while a motorist failed to understand why he

Original headline and caption from the June 10, 1969, Nashville Banner: "Readied For A Wreck—Technicians prepare a specially-rigged sports car with camera to be crashed in the opening scenes of 'The Delta Factor,' which began filming here Monday night. Several rehearsal runs were held before the early morning filming got under way." (Nashville Public Library, Nashville Room, photo by Bob Ray)

couldn't buy gas from the empty pumps. Many prominent locals with more sense appeared in the film. It was a big event.

But the times were changing, as evidenced by the film we saw called "Where It's At." It played at the Loew's Crescent at 415 Church St. and was billed as "a '60s comedy where moral and ethical standards collide." They did indeed.

We drove over to the grand old Melrose Theater on Franklin Pike in Berry Hill and took in another reflection of the period, the controversial "Midnight Cowboy." If you didn't like the show you could always knock down a few pins at their famous bowling alley right next door. It was a nice setup.

Our group was made up of a few friends who were married at the time but still "double dated" on occasion to the drive-in movie theaters (see Chapter 1). One of our last escapades was in June at the Warner Park on Highway 70. The couple we went with, combined with a double feature of "Destroy All Monsters" and "Brute and the Beast," made for a forgettable night. The only redeeming factor was that I had a great "date."

Not at the theater but beamed directly into homes in July was the first landing of a man on the moon. It enthralled our family as we sat for hours by the television watching the proceedings. Talk about change—this was amazing stuff.

Lifestyles were on the move, too. The hippie subculture and anti-establishment movement were big among many kids. The Sharon Tate murders committed by Charles Manson and his dysfunctional, communal psychos put us on edge. Ted Kennedy was stammering to explain the drowning of Mary Jo Kopechne in his car, while locally the trial

"Where It's At," a film released in 1969, played in Nashville at the Loew's Crescent Theater on Church Street.

of William Powell for the murder of Haynie Gourley was underway, which affected my parents. The Gourleys were good friends. I distinctly recall seeing Mrs. Gourley in tears at our home on more than one occasion.

Music went from soul and rock 'n' roll sounds to the drug-infused tunes of the hippie generation. A new culture was moving in. Led Zepplin topped the charts and groups with bizarre songs and names surfaced. Iron Butterfly, Canned Heat, Jefferson Airplane, Mothers of Invention were going strong, and King Crimson released one that year called "21st Century Schizoid Man." The Who with "We're not Gonna Take It" made their mark.

Meanwhile, the old soul sounds attempted to hang on. The Temptations tried to stay relevant with "Psychedelic Shack," but Marvin Gaye, Junior Walker and the All Stars, Mel and Tim ("Backfield in Motion"), James Brown, The Chairman of the Board ("Give Me Just a Little More Time"), and

Mahi Mahi was a Polynesian-themed restaurant located on White Bridge Road.

Brooke Benton's "A Rainy Night in Georgia" all stayed the course. Within a decade most of that sound had faded away.

Rock festivals had exploded a couple of years earlier, culminating with Woodstock in August 1969 proclaiming the mantra of "Peace and Love." It changed everything. The first pop-music festival of this sort ever held in the mid-south was in Fayetteville, Tenn., the same month. It mainly featured local combos and recording artists such as Lemonade Charades, Clifford Curry ("She Shot a Hole in My Soul"), The Rocking Rebellions, Charlie McCoy, The Fairlanes and Robert Knight, to name a few.

At about the same time the hippie-oriented "Free Nashville Music Festival" was held at Centennial Park. The lineup included The Jerms, Neon Philharmonic and Bubble Puppy, among others, and attracted a diverse crowd. It eventually was discontinued over security issues. Too much peace and love going on, I suppose.

Graduation came and went. My wife's sister Joan ended her reign at Hillsboro, and Carolyn got her degree at Peabody despite being disrupted by a rainstorm spawned by hurricane Camille. My parents, in her honor, took us to dine at the new Hawaiian restaurant on White Bridge Road called Mahi Mahi, a wonderful seafood spot. The only problem was that I was asked to leave because I came without a tie—a "no-no" at Mahi Mahi. After a quick trip home for my clip-on, I was whisked right on in by the management and avoided further embarrassment to all. My folks gave my new graduate a brand new Singer Touch and Sew sewing machine for all of her hard work. She needed it, for I tore up my clothes on a regular basis.

As for me, I received news that Memphis State University had accepted my application for the fall. What a shock, considering my Animal House-like grade-point average and behavior four years earlier in Florida.

When I got the notice in the mail our yardman, Lloyd Stokes, was the only one home to tell. It was Wednesday and he was setting up for my mom's bible class. He seemed pleased.

Our die was cast. August 23 arrived and the trek to Bluff City began. We loaded a Hertz truck and said our good-byes. I drove with my wife and our new puppy, Bogie, all jammed in the front of the cab. My ever-thoughtful parents followed, one driving our Volkswagen and the other in their own car. We had the perfect place picked out at the Yorktown Apartments in the Raleigh area of town. The No. 13 over the door was probably why it was one of the only vacancies in the complex. It was good luck for us. No triskaidekaphobia here.

After unloading, we waved to my parents as a final picture was taken commemorating the moment. It was a long period of adjustment but we were finally on our own.

As the group Chicago sang in 1969, it was "only the beginning, only just the start." What a ride it would be.

CHAPTER 27

Bus Rides and
B-Movies

IN THE 1930s, Ward DeWitt and his friend Hal Lackey frequently rode the electric streetcars downtown for 7 cents to see mostly cowboy picture shows at the Knickerbocker and Princess theaters. Afterward they re-boarded and rode to the end of the line at Cedar Lane and Belmont Boulevard. Ward had more than a mile to his house on Observatory Drive, while Hal had to go one block farther. Two decades later, my own public transit adventures would mirror theirs.

The last streetcar passed through the transfer station on Jan. 27, 1941, and Southern Coach Lines became the ruling authority for city bus service, charging only 5-cent fares. It ceased operation Nov. 30, 1952, giving way to Nashville Transit Company, upon which I did most of my riding.

I was a most fortunate child for a number of reasons, but to be able to catch the city bus just across from my side door, at the corner of Westmont and Cantrell, was exceptional. In 1956, direct service came into being, which included the Bowling-Westmont route. My friends and I became regular passengers for Saturday adventures of a bus ride to town for the picture shows.

Street poles were marked with

A Johnson Fare Box where bus tokens and coins were inserted, circa 1955.(Alex Slabosky)

A Nashville city bus bound for the Sylan Park area is decked out in advertising for Sunbeam bread, circa 1955. (Nashville Metro Archives)

a yellow ring to designate bus stops. The anticipation of waiting for the bus to round the corner was exciting. We could hear it coming two blocks away when accelerating from Woodlawn onto Lynnbrook. As it turned on to Westmont we would push each other and say "Here it comes!" It stopped with a distinctive hissing noise and the opening of tall double doors. A pleasant fellow would welcome us aboard.

We would drop our 15 cents or the equivalent in bus tokens into a rectangular metal box upon which was a glass receptacle whereby the fares would disappear down the middle making a "ching" sound until they hit the bottom. There was a circular attachment with a node on the outside of the box that went around and around even after we had made the deposit. I had no idea what that was for. I assume if this device detected a slug the motion would cease immediately and we would be asked to re-up.

Before we could take a seat, the driver would take off, prompting us to grab the tall steel poles to keep from falling into some stranger's lap. Long silver poles also stretched the length of the bus for use by those standing.

Seating capacity ranged from 33 to 41 passengers. The loud noise of the

This circa 1956 view of 6th Avenue North (looking north at Church Street) includes the Knickerbocker Theater on the left being passed by a city bus. The marque advertises "Hot-Rod Girl" and "Girls in Prison." The Hermitage Hotel can be glimpsed in the background, just beyond the theater, along with the Andrew Jackson Hotel. On the right is a Levy's men's clothier and a Harvey's department store with its trademark carousel horses. (Nashville Metro Archives)

engine, the accompanying fumes flowing through the open windows of the non-air-conditioned ride and the swaying were all part of the experience. The seats were pretty spartan, but the view was great, as we were higher up than in a car, and the numerous windows gave us views we normally didn't see.

I remember looking at the inside advertising that surrounded the entire interior just above the windows. Rusty-looking rectangular boxes placed between each window displayed schedules and were where promotion materials were inserted.

Then there was the all-important rope that stretched along both sides just above the windows. When pulled, a subdued but clearly audible bell rang, alerting the driver someone wanted to get off at the next stop. Being mischievous we would often quickly jerk the cord and jump back in our seats. The driver would always stop at the next designated area. This could only be done if the bus was full, to make it difficult to identify the culprits. Too much of this aggravation would result in a threat to take names and call parents.

Nashville Transit Company received the highest safety award in the industry in 1953–'54 and second place from 1955–'58, otherwise my parents would have had second thoughts about letting me ride. In 1956 it was crowded, as mothers availed themselves of the new "Baby Buster" program that provided free use of strollers at the newly-constructed Memorial Square Transfer Station. This shelter went into full operation at Union and Capitol Boulevard in January 1956 (see photo on page 186). It was a big promotion similar to the Stop and Shop service instituted by NTC President Carmack Cochran in 1957. Other promotions saw ads covering the entire bus to market certain products. Bernard Evers' Sunbeam Bread Company comes to mind (see photo on previous page).

I was excited on the way downtown because of all the theaters and wondering what the marquees and posters were displaying. However, the anticipation they conjured up was often let down by the actual presentation. Most of the flicks at the 5th Avenue Theater fit that description.

One of my favorite theaters was the Knickerbocker, known as Wasserman's Knickerbocker years earlier. It was located at 210 Capitol Blvd., just down the street from the bus shelter. My neighbor Alex had a family friend, Louis Rubenstein, whom he referred to as Uncle Lou, who was manager there and probably let us in for free on occasion. The theater ran straight through to 6th Avenue, so entering from that side you came in behind the screen. Pretty neat. Only 30 years earlier, in 1926, it was the first in the city to show a movie with sound. Unfortunately, it closed in 1961 but not before it had shown such Oscar-worthy movies as "Hot-Rod Girl" and "Girls in Prison." I was not allowed to stay for those.

I did stay for the classic "Attack of the Crab Monsters" and "Not of This Earth" that played there in 1957. I used to catch crabs in a basket off a pier on family vacations, so the crab movie particularly appealed to me, though crab nightmares were not uncommon afterwards.

"Attack of the 50 Foot Woman" was laughable, which is what we did during most of that film. The second part of that double feature in November 1958 was "War of the Satellites."

In 1959 "Go Johnny Go," featuring deejay Alan Freed and teenage-heartthrob Jimmy Clanton, graced the screen. His hit song "Just a Dream" was huge. It was the second time I had seen young girls scream at a singer

*The Memorial Square Transfer Station bus shelter at Capitol Boulevard and Union Street is show
soon after opening in January 1956. The Hermitage Hotel is on the left and the YMCA building
is on the right. Today this location is near the Korean War Monument on War Memorial Plaza.*
(Nashville Public Library, The Nashville Room, photo by Bob White)

in a theater. The other time was during "Love Me Tender" with Elvis at the
Paramount in November 1956. I thought it was stupid, but what did I know?
I was a boy.

"Go Johnny Go" featured Chuck Berry, The Big Bopper ("Chantilly
Lace") and Richie Valens ("Oh Donna" and "LaBamba") among others. I
guess the deaths of Bopper and Valens in a plane crash with Buddy Holly
earlier that year made it even more popular, plus the added attraction was a
"3 Stooges-Fun-o-rama," which sealed the deal for kids my age.

In 1957, "I was a Teenage Werewolf" starring Michael Landon and "I was
a Teenage Frankenstein" played together. To see a werewolf in a high-school
letter jacket was comical. In 1961 I ordered a mask from "Horror Monster
Magazine" that looked identical to what the monster wore in "Teenage
Frankenstein." It was on the cover of the second issue, and for years I used it
on Halloween to scare kids.

In the waning days of the theater in 1960, science fiction ruled with such
time-honored gems as "12 to the Moon" and "Battle in Outer Space." It was
B-movie heaven.

The address 415 Church St. was home to the Princess Theater until the name was changed in 1959 when a Cinerama screen was installed. The Princess Gift and Fun shop next door was an added lure for us prior to the movie. We always went in there. The Crescent Cinerama in December of that year was introduced with a film by the famous Lowell Thomas. Between 1949 and 1962 some unflatteringly referred to the theater as the Princess Double Feature.

Paul Clements recollects that he and I caught the bus from the Belle Meade Theater to see horror master Vincent Price in "The House of Wax" and "The House on Haunted Hill." Both were eerily chilling. He claims I constantly screamed during those classics. I, on the other hand, am highly suspect of that but am unable to refute it. In "House on Haunted Hill" some poor employee of the theater was placed in charge of pulling a skeleton-like prop on a wire (which was to give the appearance of it coming out of the screen) over the audience to the projection booth above the balcony. Bits of it fell in route, lessening the effect, plus the black box it came out of was visible on stage. It was fun to see, and the crowds seemed to enjoy it. I did see a Sugar Daddy whistle by its skull, evidently thrown by a villainous teen.

There were plenty of shrieks during the showing of another Price classic, called "The Tingler," in 1959. I had been forewarned there were vibration devices attached under selected seats, which was true. There was a lot of screaming when the catch phrase "Scream, scream for your lives" was uttered by Price. When the lobster-like creature

The bus routed often taken by the author went past the 3400 block of West End and under the railroad bridge (since replaced by Interstate 440). Photo is circa 1955. (Nashville Metro Archives)

was to attack and escape into the crowd, devices planted throughout the venue magnified the sound effect. Additionally, you could see a string pulling the creature from its cage while it was escaping. This drastically reduced the terror level.

A longtime grade-school friend named Clifton conjured a way to disrupt a movie and irritate the ushers one Saturday at the Princess. I went as his accomplice. He had concealed a can of Campbell's condensed Cream of Mushroom Soup within his overcoat. Clifton was a big kid and one heck of a football player back then in the late 1950s, so it was well hidden. There seemed to be a large audience that day as we made our way through the lobby, past the rest rooms, then up the few stairs to the near-empty balcony. As we made our way down to the rail overlooking the main floor, the hearty soup was brought out from under the overcoat and opened. At a precise moment, during a particularly touching scene, we both leaned over the rail, emitted a guttural, regurgitating noise and poured the gelatinous, chunky mixture upon the viewers below.

Removing our faces quickly from sight we could hear cries of "OH, MY GOSH!" and "GOOD GRACIOUS!" among numerous profanities being thrown about. We stealthily made our way back down the steps, peered through the curtain to the main floor and witnessed confusion, followed by two ushers hurrying to the impact area with a couple of yellow pails, flashlights and a mop. We overheard a patron say that some kids became ill in the balcony, at which time one of the ushers (an older gentleman) mumbled an obscenity and proceeded to make his way up the steps.

Unable to contain our laughter any longer, we quickly scurried out on to Church Street and disappeared into the crowds of weekend shoppers.

After a day at the movies, full of popcorn, candy, fun and vivid cinema memories, time was of the essence as the Bowling-Westmont bus departed soon from shelter C at the transfer station. We would hustle several blocks back to Union and begin looking at each bus, intently reading the banner displayed in the window. Once ours arrived, we felt relief.

The 25-minute ride home took us back down Broad past the huge Coke sign at the split of 21st Avenue and West End. We went by Tarbox School, the Allen Hotel and Mrs. Martha's restaurant. The excitement level of the day would have diminished somewhat, so we just gazed out of the windows. There was Vanderbilt all on the left, Firestone where my Dad had his first job, Centennial Park, the Hippodrome Roller Rink, Patterson's Esso, Henry Drugs, Candyland and rows of apartment complexes. I remember Albertine Maxwell's Dance Studio and further down a fire station. Gus Drug and Schwartz's Delicatessen were on the right after passing under the Tennessee Central Railway trestle. It was always fun if a train was moving overhead. The Jewish Community Center followed as we made a left onto Bowling Avenue beside Elmington Park and West End High School.

By this time we were the last of the passengers. A right onto Woodlawn, a left on Lynnbrook and a right on Westmont brought my backyard court lights into view. Standing up I pulled the rope, in earnest this time; the bell rang, and we walked to the front. It was the end of the line. As we held onto the stainless steel pole by the driver and swung down the steps as the double doors opened, he would usually say "See ya, boys." We would said "See ya," and step off. Away the bus would go, over the hill at Wilson, and disappear, leaving only a cloudy plume of smoke.

Just as Ward DeWitt and Hal Lackey had done some 20 years earlier, we also began our journey home, only this time home was right there across the street. How times had changed. How fortunate we were.

CHAPTER 28

A Childhood Home

When crickets call my heart is ever yearning,
Once more to be returning, Home.
And, though fortune may forsake me,
Sweet dreams will ever take me, Home
— Vic Damone, "Home" (1961)

IN FEBRUARY of 1940 my parents, Tom and Bay Henderson, moved with their two young daughters from Cherokee Avenue to a home built in 1938 by C.E and Annette Pavelka Hagstrom at 700 Cantrell Ave., between Woodmont Boulevard and Woodlawn Drive in the Woodmont Hills section of town. The house was non-existent just three years earlier when the Hagstroms purchased the lot from Sperry Realty Company.

The 54 acres of the Cantrell estates were mostly open areas of grassy fields, but had recently been apportioned off into lots for eventual home construction. Woodmont School was just two blocks away, and its reputation was beginning to attract new home buyers with young children.

Our large two-story home sat on a small hill. It had a big backyard, close proximity to the school and was directly across the street from a huge lot called Herbert's Field where cows grazed and school kids played ball. It was a natural fit for our family. They turned the new home into a wonderful gathering and nurturing place for countless neighborhood kids and families for over a half century.

The next year WWII would erupt, sending men off to war. For many this fight directly affected local communities, from the parents who ran the PTA at our schools, to our teachers, to those who freely played on the playgrounds

Tom and Bay Henderson in 1942.

and in lots like Herbert's Field.

My father became a navy captain and was gone for months on end. My mother's beloved brother, Wilson Lynch, volunteered and was killed in action just as the war was ending. She did her part in the war effort by starting a backyard victory garden and continued it after her brother's death. Our country needed large amounts of food to supply troops and every homeowner was encouraged to help in some fashion. These gardens sprouted up all over the country. My sisters would often take their little wagon around the block, selling the bounty to folks around the neighborhood. My sister Beth said Mom made her go back to a lady who "did not pay you enough." This was no time to be cheap. Tending to the garden, harvesting the crops and selling the produce were not easy tasks, but my mother was determined to stay connected with loved ones in the trenches. It was the least she could do.

After the war ended, my father returned home and noticed that many local children tended to congregate across the street in Herbert's Field as soon as school would let out. He decided to offer to coach those kids in all sports.

As a three-sport star at Vanderbilt, his intentions were received with open arms by the school parents.

Though my mother was still producing fruits and vegetables, my father envisioned a badminton/ basketball court in the garden's plot of land to benefit neighborhood children. Having daughters who were athletically inclined, he figured it would benefit them as well. After much discus-

In this 1953 photo some neighbors gather on the family court (left to right): Henry Hurt, the author's sister, Lynn, Julie Foley and Tommy Frist. The author stands in front with a basketball.

sion, my mother relented and the project began. Johnny Herbert realized his wooden goals were not ideal in his field, so he dug them up and gave

them to my dad. Mr. Herbert also provided a mule, a scoop, some concrete from Herbert Materials and leftover clay bricks from finished jobs. So began the work with my father to build what would become a magnet for area children.

A 48-foot-by-24-foot concrete court was laid out and christened with an inscription, written into the wet concrete, bearing my sisters' names: "Beth, Lynn, July 7 1945." Two large light poles were installed

Johnny Herbert and his son, Charlie, remove the old wooden goal posts to instal metal ones. Charlie was tragically killed shortly thereafter in a traffic accident.

At left, the author watches the "big kids" play basketball on his family's backyard court in 1956. His father installed a shorter goal (background) so that little kids could play, too. At right, the author's father provides pointers as his son takes a shot on a big goal in 1957.

that made the court available for night play. Those lights served as a beacon in the evening sky, indicating to neighborhood kids that there was action going on at the Henderson's court.

The following year I came along. In the 1950s I remember watching older boys and girls play ball for hours as I sat in awe of those "big kids." My sisters, while in high school at Hillsboro, always had boys around from both Hillsboro and MBA. There were so many wanting to play ball that late arrivers had to wait their turns while sitting in the grass and in chairs my mother had set out.

As I became old enough to dribble, my father built a small wooden goal so I could get the ball up to the basket. It, in turn, attracted my grade school friends.

In 1955, the old wooden

By 1966 the author (middle) had become a "big kid" along with his friend Paul Clements (right). Neighborhood tournaments were regularly organized.

goals that were given to us by Johnny Herbert were replaced with metal ones and installed by him and his son, Charlie. It was a big event.

Over the years hundreds of neighborhood kids of all ages continued to play on that court. In 1989, Dad's court was named "Best Backyard Basketball Court" in Nashville by H. Jackson Brown Jr.'s book "Nashville's Best." I am glad my dad was around to see it named as such.

Our home was an escape for many and a place where parents felt completely comfortable letting their children come. One parent queried her daughter, "Where are you going?" The child replied, "I am going to the Hendersons." "Okay," said the mom.

My sisters eventually moved on to college, and I became the "big kid" with friends. Now other little kids who came to play had to sit and watch. This chain of events continued decade after decade. I organized basketball tournaments there for many years, played whiffle ball games in the summer, honed my badminton skills, and often watched my father get up from his chair inside the house, after observing a non-coordinated kid shoot the basketball, and say, "That kid needs some help." Outside he would go to instruct.

Needless to say, I wore out countless pairs of Chuck Taylor Converse tennis shoes out there.

I was privileged in the early 1960s to have seen my brother-in-law-to-be, dressed in tux with taps on his patent leather shoes, come out to the court

At left is one of the many backyard picnics that took place by the court, this one in 1970. At right, the author's wife, Carolyn (standing), and son enjoy the backyard at a 1973 family gathering. On the left edge is the author's father.

The author, his father and his Great Aunt Irene Wilson have dinner on the patio of the home in 1959.

prior to picking up my sister on a big date. A friend and I were just shooting around and he said, "Let me show you how it is done." Not a great basketball player either, he took two dribbles, drove to the basket and just as he was laying the ball up his feet shot out from under him. The ball went flying as he collided with the base of the metal goal in a groin-cringing, straddling move that I have yet to see duplicated. Clutching himself he said, "I have to go."

My own kids eventually played on the court, as did countless other "Henderson Graduates."

Pickup games in the summer would prompt my mother and/or father to bring out a bizarre concoction of Kool-Aid and who knows what else. It was the subject of much discussion.

Late in his life my dad got children involved in Pickle Ball, similar to badminton but with paddles and a hard ball designed for reduced distance.

The court was the main attraction of our backyard but not the only one. Hundreds of family pictures are inscribed with the word "backyard." We had picnics there and neighbors would gather, walking through backyards nearby. Hedgerows containing gaps for entering into other folks' property surrounded our yard. Through one of those gaps was the Haurys' field where a see-saw was just waiting to be played upon. It was a time of friendliness; everyone knew each other and fences were almost non-existent. We played "out" at night with our backyard hackberry used as a home base.

Erected in the early 1940s, we also had an expansive, iron, double swing set that entertained both children and adults. My mother, at the time in her 70s, was swinging with the grandchildren when the chain broke, sending her into space and abruptly back down to earth, breaking her collarbone. The kids raced over and said, "Are you okay, Nana?" To which she replied, "I am fine, now go get your grandfather."

When football practice ended in Herbert's Field, a massive exodus of players crossed Westmont Avenue through our gravel driveway and around to our backyard to a "hose pipe" attached to the water spicket for a cooling drink. Water was potable back then.

After I got married and had children, our family picnicked in the backyard with Mom providing the nourishment. My father taught my youngest son golf by letting him hit plastic balls around that huge hackberry tree occupying a large part of the yard. Where once a little playhouse sat for my sisters,

The Henderson family celebrates New Year's Eve 1974 in the playroom at 700 Cantrell Avenue. Front row (left to right): Carolyn Henderson (wife) and Lynn White (sister). On couch: Vance Wheeler (nephew), Amy Wheeler (niece), Genevieve Selph (mother-in-law) and Kathy Wheeler (niece). Back row: Hal Selph (brother-in-law), Bay Henderson (mother), the author, and Doug White (brother-in-law).

leaves were burned every fall in a concrete barbeque pit that replaced it. We washed cars, shot off fireworks, and Mom still had a small flower bed she tended.

Our house was host to a family wedding, a sister's wedding reception, my pre-marital party, and countless birthday and holiday gatherings.

My parents provided a room and served meals for the Billy Graham Crusade in 1954 and made available our home to exchange students as well. My wife and I lived there in 1969 after my stint in the military.

The patio in our home's center section was a favorite dining, bird-feeding, flower-growing and grilling area. In the playroom, Mom hosted a regular Wednesday Bible class featuring Mrs. Whittemore, whose WNAH radio program, "Bible Class of the Air," was broadcast worldwide. We hung out there, too. We shot pool, operated a movie theater, played records on the hi-fi, had dates over and watched shows like "Shock Theater" late at night.

Mom was a constant source of counseling for neighborhood kids, frequently citing scripture or just giving timely advice in the breakfast room.

Memories of sliding down the banister, hearing Dad stoke the furnace in the basement and seeing Mom hang clothes on the line in our side yard were

The family celebrates the 75th birthday of Tom Henderson in 1987.

all part of life at 700 Cantrell Ave. Growing up there and being raised by such wonderful parents was an indescribable gift.

A noted shift in our neighborhood began back in the early 1970s, as desegregation busing took a toll on Woodmont School. Land values increased and new housing eventually swallowed up playground lots like Herbert's Field. Fences began to replace the hedges and security for the first time became a concern. The quiet streets of the 1950s and '60s once surrounding the area had become more traffic-laden in the 1980s and 1990s. With our neighborhood school eventually disappearing and lots like the Haury's and Herbert's Field now gone, children tended to stay home. Those days when dogs followed children on their bikes to school, and kids played in local fields, rode to our court, pedaled to Moon Drugs or the Belle Meade Theater, all unsupervised, became ancient history.

My sisters and I moved on, but my folks continued to welcome kids to their home to play on the basketball court. Mom still gave invaluable advice. Dad continued to push mow his yard although just a little at a time. Picture-taking of the beautiful dogwood tree and those taken "in the backyard" ended by the late 1990s as Tom and Bay Henderson, both age 88, began to change as well. Health issues finally forced them to move. The inevitable occurred in February 2001 when our home place was put on the market and sold to a young professional couple.

In 2005 it was sold again but this time to a developer who saw dollar signs over historical value. Due to poor zoning regulations and lack of intervention by the city council, a new home was constructed over the entire backyard, obliterating any evidence of what had taken place there over the past 60-plus years. The hand-built court, light poles, the large iron swing set, the barbeque pit, the huge hackberry we used to swing on, the hedge rows and freshly-cut green grass my father used to mow are now just a memory.

My childhood home still remains, but its backyard and the personality it derived from my parents, and the hundreds of neighborhood children who were blessed to have visited there, are all now gone. But they left an indelible stamp, a stamp of a particular kind, one that reflected a period in America when neighbors knew and cared about each other.

As friend Paul Clements so profoundly wrote: "Mrs. Henderson's victory

One of the last photos of the house while it was owned by the Hendersons, taken in 1990.

garden was part of a national sacrifice that preserved, for a time, a way of life. … Because of that wartime sacrifice a place that once blossomed with summer vegetables was allowed to blossom with children, decade after decade, by the best kind of old-fashioned neighbors."

A historical marker should be erected.

GRATITUDES

A dictionary definition of "acknowledgement" means "to show that one has noticed." An acknowledgements page is standard in most books and is almost always used by accomplished authors to mention those who have helped them in some way to get their literary gems published. Not being an accomplished author, I have no ties to standard protocol, so I have renamed this page for my purposes. I prefer to go with "Gratitudes," which has been defined as "being thankful." To the following people I am overly thankful:

No. 1 on my list is Allen Forkum, the editor of The Nashville Retrospect newspaper. His tireless efforts in the logistical and editorial side in the publication process of this book have been over and beyond helpful. I cannot stress that enough. In addition, without his inclusions of my ramblings in the Retrospect, I firmly believe that "When I Was a Kid" would not have come to fruition. I will just say I am extremely grateful to him and his family.

No. 2 is Nashville's premier early historian and author Paul Clements. Paul is a lifelong friend. In making that statement I have taken a huge risk, but one that I am willing to take. Not only have we shared many childhood memories, but Paul has freely offered his advice and recommendations and has suggested countless topics that I otherwise might not have remembered. His referral of me to Allen gave me the forum to relate these childhood experiences. For his thoughts, insights and availability at a moment's notice, I am extremely grateful.

Thirdly, I thank Charles Nelson and Anita Coursey at the Tennessee State Library and Archives, Beth Odle at the Nashville Banner Archives at the downtown library, as well as Kenneth Feith and his crew at Metro Archives, for their invaluable cooperation, kindness and willingness to help in my research requests.

Lastly, I also thank friend and author Paul Erland, my Nashville Retrospect admirers, and other acquaintances for their continual encouragement to compile my memories and recollections into book form.

Gratitudes to all.

Tom Henderson III

Made in the USA
San Bernardino, CA
22 March 2015